Ordnance Survey
Dorset
Walks

Pathfinder Guide
Compiled by Brian Conduit

Key to colour coding

The walks are divided into three broad categories, indicated by the following colours:

Short, easy walks

Walks of moderate length, likely to involve some modest uphill walking

More challenging walks, which may be longer and/or over more rugged terrain, often with some stiff climbs

Acknowledgements

I am grateful to the following for their valuable advice and assistance: Mr P. Luxmoore (Rights of Way Assistant, Dorset County Council) and Mr I.W.S. Robertson (Land Agent for the National Trust, Wessex Region).

While every care has been taken to ensure the accuracy of the route directions, the publishers cannot accept responsibility for errors or omissions, or for changes in details given. It has to be emphasised that the countryside is not static: hedges and fences can be removed, field boundaries can alter, footpaths can be rerouted and changes of ownership can result in the closure or diversion of some concessionary paths. Also paths that are easy and pleasant for walking in fine conditions may become slippery, muddy and difficult in wet weather and stepping stones over rivers and streams may become impassable.

Ordnance Survey   ISBN 0-319-00294-2
Jarrold Publishing   ISBN 0-7117-0573-9

First published 1992 by Ordnance Survey and Jarrold Publishing

Ordnance Survey   Jarrold Publishing
Romsey Road   Whitefriars
Maybush   Norwich NR3 1TR
Southampton SO9 4DH

© Crown copyright 1992

Printed in Great Britain by Jarrold Printing, Norwich. 1/92

Contents

Introduction to Dorset

Dorset must rank as one of the most unspoilt and unchanged counties in England. Nineteenth-century and later industrialisation and urbanisation have largely passed it by and left it mercifully unscathed. It lacks any major mineral resources apart from Purbeck and Portland stone, which has been quarried since the Middle Ages. Except for the Bournemouth–Poole conurbation, there are no large towns and the county has no motorways crossing it. Dorset remains today a predominantly rural and agricultural county of small, traditional market towns and quiet, attractive villages where the pace of life seems to belong to a less frenzied age than our own.

Although Dorset may not have any motorways, there are plenty of busy main roads. Some – particularly the A35 – are thronged in summer by the cars of holiday-makers on their way to the more crowded resorts of Devon and Cornwall. As they speed through, they miss out on a region that possesses an enormous variety of inland and coastal scenery and a rich historic legacy, both contained within a relatively compact area.

Indeed, apart from the absence of high mountain ranges, Dorset has almost every conceivable type of terrain, but all on a pleasantly intimate scale: nowhere in the county is higher than 1,000 feet (305 m). Dominating the landscape are the chalk downs: open, sweeping, grassy uplands that stretch from the former forest lands of Cranborne Chase on the Wiltshire and Hampshire borders right across the middle of the county, roughly from the north-east to the south-west, to the coast. The many ridge-top tracks and footpaths that traverse these downs provide splendid walking and a succession of panoramic views.

West Dorset has a very different landscape: it is a region of rolling, steep-sided, well wooded limestone hills that cradle the fertile clay lowlands of Marshwood Vale. To the north of the chalk downs is the peaceful, lush, undulating country of Blackmoor Vale, watered by the gently-flowing River Stour and its various tributaries. To the south, reaching down to the Frome valley and Poole Harbour, are the remnants of the once-extensive heathland that covered much of south-east Dorset. Although now partly covered by conifer plantations and encroached upon by farmland, army tank-ranges and the suburban sprawl of Bournemouth, enough remains of the heathland to enable us to appreciate why Dorset's most famous son, Thomas Hardy, who was born on the edge of the 'Great Heath', found this combination of woodland, grassland, heather, gorse and scrub so fascinating and strangely mysterious.

Surrounded by water on three sides – the River Frome and Poole Harbour to the north and the English Channel to the east and south – and therefore almost detached from the mainland is the Isle of Purbeck. With its mixture of clay, limestone and chalk, Purbeck is a virtual microcosm of the rest of Dorset. The northern part is a continuation of the heathland and forests that extend across the Frome estuary and Poole Harbour. The south is limestone country, where the austere and open landscape of bright green fields criss-crossed by drystone walls is reminiscent of the dales of Derbyshire and Yorkshire, apart from the proximity of the sea. In this region

The historic village of Abbotsbury, cradled amidst rolling downs

are to be found the remains of the once-flourishing quarrying industry, much of the Purbeck stone being shipped via Swanage to London and beyond. The most distinctive features of this area are the Purbeck Hills, a chalk ridge running across the middle of the peninsula from around Lulworth to the Old Harry Rocks at the tip of Ballard Down, broken only by the gap occupied by the dramatic ruins of Corfe Castle.

Corfe, the finest and indeed one of the few medieval castles in the county, is a part of Dorset's historic legacy, which is dominated by the remains of prehistory. No walker can fail to be aware of the numerous hill-forts, tumuli and other ancient monuments that litter much of the landscape. Dorset, along with neighbouring Wiltshire and Hampshire, was one of the most heavily populated regions of prehistoric England, the drier slopes of the chalk uplands being preferred by early settlers to the damp, marshy and thickly-forested lowlands. Predominant among the many hill-forts is Maiden Castle, a massive defensive complex and chief stronghold of the Durotriges tribe. In AD 69 the Durotriges suffered a devastating defeat here at the hands of the Roman invaders; later the fort faded into comparative obscurity as the Romans established their new administrative headquarters of Durnovaria — modern Dorchester — in the valley below.

Many of the other hill-forts included in the walks in this book are equally impressive, even if on a smaller scale, less elaborate and less well known. Lambert's Castle and Coney's Castle occupy adjacent hills in the west of the county overlooking Marshwood Vale and Lyme Bay. A short distance to the east are the beech-clad slopes of Lewesdon Hill. Eggardon Hill, perhaps the most atmospheric of all, broods over the surviving

woodlands of the medieval Powerstock Forest. The triangular Abbotsbury Castle overlooks Chesil Beach, while Flower's Barrow commands spectacular views above Worbarrow Bay on the Purbeck coast. Badbury Rings, a particularly fine and extensive fort, is situated in the midst of sweeping downland near the junction of two Roman roads. At Dorset's most easterly point, the Double Dykes defend the landward approach to Hengistbury Head overlooking Christchurch Harbour.

Many would argue that the most striking, and definitely the most unusual, of Dorset's prehistoric monuments is the Cerne Giant, an aggressively virile figure of a man cut into the chalk hillside above Cerne Abbas — almost certainly a fertility symbol. One of the most impressive earthworks, Bokerley Ditch, which runs for 4 miles (6.5 km) along the north-eastern boundary of the county, is not of prehistoric origin at all but a Romano-British construction of the fourth century AD, probably built as a defence against Saxon invaders. It obviously was not successful, as Dorset became incorporated within the Saxon kingdom of Wessex. The latter was almost a forgotten name until resurrected in the novels of Thomas Hardy and is now virtually synonymous with the county.

In a region noted for the intimacy of its landscape, it is perhaps fitting that most of Dorset's historic buildings — apart from the overwhelming collection of prehistoric remains — are similarly intimate and on a small scale, rather than grand and imposing. There are some notable exceptions: Corfe Castle has already been mentioned; Christchurch Priory can claim to be the finest non-cathedral church in the country; and there are impressive abbeys at Sherborne and Milton. But there are no great cathedrals and no extensive monastic remains to rival those of Yorkshire or the Scottish Borders. Dorset's parish churches are not as imposing as those of East Anglia or the Cotswolds, and there are no country houses on the scale of Chatsworth, Woburn or Blenheim.

Although there are, nevertheless, many fine churches and attractive manor houses, it is not so much individually outstanding buildings as overall appearance and architectural harmony that makes the towns and villages of Dorset so appealing. Few counties can boast a finer collection of towns than Lyme Regis, Sherborne, Shaftesbury, Wareham, Blandford Forum, Bridport, Wimborne Minster and Dorchester itself. As for villages, the list could be very long, but of those visited in the course of the walks in this book perhaps Cerne Abbas, Powerstock, Abbotsbury, Worth Matravers, Milton Abbas and Ashmore can be singled out.

It is impossible to think of Dorset without

The extensive Iron Age fort of Badbury Rings

considering Thomas Hardy, whose 'Wessex' novels are so interwoven with the landscape of his native county. Born in a small cottage at Higher Bockhampton in 1840, Hardy lived most of his life in Dorset and died at his home just outside Dorchester in 1928. His ashes are in Westminster Abbey, but his heart lies in Stinsford churchyard, a short distance from his birthplace, amidst the countryside he loved and which inspired so much of his writing.

Hardy's long life overlapped with three widely differing developments that have had a major impact on the Dorset scene: tourism, military occupation and forestry. The discovery of the pleasures of sea-bathing by eighteenth-century royalty and aristocracy led to the early rise of Lyme Regis and Weymouth as fashionable resorts, followed by Swanage in the early nineteenth century, though all were overshadowed by the rapid growth of Bournemouth in the Victorian era. Fortunately most of Dorset's resorts have remained relatively small, and the county has largely avoided the rash of housing and commercial development that has blighted some other stretches of coastline.

During the First and Second World Wars, the army took over parts of Dorset's heathland and a large stretch of the Purbeck coast for tank-training purposes. Despite some ugly scars left by tank tracks, this long period of military occupation has had the unforeseen bonus of preserving the landscape from modern intensive farming practices. Since 1974, the Ministry of Defence has allowed restricted access to this fascinating area and developed well way-marked routes for walkers.

Hardy did not live to see the extensive conifer plantations of Wareham and Puddletown Forests that have appeared since the 1920s, smothering much of his 'Great Heath' and bringing about a more drastic and permanent change to the landscape than anything done by the army. But there are gains as well as losses, for the Forestry Commission welcomes walkers into its forests and provides car parks, picnic areas and waymarked trails.

Dorset has much to offer the walker. Perhaps the main attraction is the coast; spectacular, varied, strenuous in places and offering a whole series of interesting features: Golden Cap (the highest point on the south coast of England), Chesil Beach, Durdle Door, Lulworth Cove and the Old Harry Rocks. Much of the coast is owned and protected by the National Trust, and for almost the whole of its length it is traversed by the South West Coast Path and excellently waymarked. Inland the chalk downs, with their exhilarating ridge-top views and dry valley bottoms, may be the chief magnet, but the walker can also choose from the hills of west Dorset, the gentle and placid scenery of Blackmoor Vale, the isolated remnants of heathland in the eastern part of the county, the sweeping vistas of the former hunting ground of Cranborne Chase, and the varied attractions of the Isle of Purbeck. Some of the less-used footpaths in the more remote parts of the county may be less well maintained and waymarked than elsewhere; some overgrown and muddy sections may be encountered and greater care will be needed with route-finding.

Nowhere are you likely to be too far from a village or small town with a welcoming pub or tearoom, an additional pleasure of walking in Dorset.

The National Trust

Anyone who likes visiting places of natural beauty and/or historic interest has cause to be grateful to the National Trust. Without it, many such places would probably have vanished by now, either under an avalanche of concrete and bricks and mortar or through reservoir construction or blanket afforestation.

It was in response to the pressures on the countryside posed by the relentless march of Victorian industrialisation that the Trust was set up in 1895. Its founders, inspired by the common goals of protecting and conserving Britain's national heritage and widening public access to it, were Sir Robert Hunter, Octavia Hill and Canon Rawnsley; a solicitor, a social reformer and a clergyman respectively. The latter was particularly influential. As a canon of Carlisle Cathedral and vicar of Crosthwaite (near Keswick), he was concerned about threats to the Lake District and had already been active in protecting footpaths and promoting public access to open countryside. After the flooding of Thirlmere in 1879 to create a large reservoir, he and his two colleagues became increasingly convinced that the only effective protection was outright ownership of land.

The purpose of the National Trust is to preserve areas of natural beauty and sites of historic interest by acquisition, holding them in trust for the nation and making them available for public access and enjoyment. Some of its properties have been acquired through purchase, but many have been donated. Nowadays it is not only one of the biggest landowners in the country, but also one of the most active conservation charities, protecting well over half a million acres of land, including over 500 miles of coastline and a large number of historic properties (houses, castles and gardens) in England, Wales and Northern Ireland. (There is a separate National Trust for Scotland, which was set up in 1931.)

Furthermore, once a piece of land has come under Trust ownership, it is difficult for its status to be altered. As a result of Parliamentary legislation in 1907, the Trust was given the right to declare its property inalienable, so ensuring that in any dispute it can appeal directly to Parliament.

As it works towards its dual aims of conserving areas of attractive countryside and encouraging greater public access (not easy to reconcile in this age of mass tourism), the Trust provides an excellent service to walkers by creating new concessionary paths and waymarked trails, by maintaining stiles and footbridges and by combating the ever-increasing problem of footpath erosion.

For details of membership, contact the National Trust at the address on page 78.

The Ramblers' Association

No organisation works more actively to protect and extend the rights and interests of walkers in the countryside than the Ramblers' Association. Its aims (summarised here) are clear: to foster a greater knowledge, love and care of the countryside; to assist in the protection and enhancement of public rights of way and areas of natural beauty; to work for greater public access to the countryside and to encourage more people to take up rambling as a healthy, recreational activity.

It was founded in 1935 when, following the setting up of a National Council of Ramblers' Federation in 1931, a number of federations earlier formed in London, Manchester, the Midlands and elsewhere came together to create a more effective pressure group, to deal with such contemporary problems as the disappearance and obstruction of footpaths, the prevention of access to open mountain and moorland and increasing hostility from landowners. This was the era of the mass trespasses, when there were sometimes violent confrontations between ramblers and gamekeepers, especially on the moorlands of the Peak District.

Since then the Ramblers' Association has played an influential role in preserving and developing the national footpath network, supporting the creation of National Parks and encouraging the designation and way-marking of long-distance footpaths.

Our freedom to walk in the countryside is precarious, and requires constant vigilance. As well as the perennial problems of footpaths being illegally obstructed, disappearing through lack of use or extinguished by housing or road construction, new dangers can spring up at any time.

It is to meet such problems and dangers that the Ramblers' Association exists and represents the interests of all walkers. The address to write to for information on the Ramblers' Association and how to become a member is given on page 78.

The fine tower of Beaminster church

Walkers and the law

The average walker in a National Park or other popular walking area, armed with the appropriate Ordnance Survey map, reinforced perhaps by a guidebook giving detailed walking instructions, is unlikely to run into legal difficulties, but it is useful to know something about the law relating to public rights of way. The right to walk over certain parts of the countryside has developed over a long period of time, and how such rights came into being and how far they are protected by the law is a complex subject, fascinating in its own right, but too lengthy to be discussed here. The following comments are intended simply to be a helpful guide, backed up by the Countryside Access Charter, a concise summary of walkers' rights and obligations drawn up by the Countryside Commission.

Basically there are two main kinds of public rights of way: footpaths (for walkers only) and bridleways (for walkers, riders on horseback and pedal cyclists). Footpaths and bridleways are shown by broken green lines on Ordnance Survey Pathfinder and Outdoor Leisure maps and broken red lines on Landranger maps. There is also a third category, called byways or 'roads used as a public path': chiefly broad, walled tracks (green lanes) or farm roads, which walkers, riders and cyclists have to share, usually only occasionally, with motor vehicles. Many of these public paths have been in existence for hundreds of years and some even originated as prehistoric trackways and have been in constant use for well over 2,000 years.

The term 'right of way' means exactly what it says. It gives right of passage over what, in the vast majority of cases, is private land, and you are required to keep to the line of the path and not stray onto the land either side. If you inadvertently wander off the right of way — either because of faulty map-reading or because the route is not clearly indicated on the ground — you are technically trespassing and the wisest course is to ask the nearest available person (farmer or fellow walker) to direct you back to the correct route. There are stories of unpleasant confrontations between walkers and farmers at times, but in general most farmers are helpful and co-operative when responding to a genuine and polite request for assistance in route finding.

Obstructions can sometimes be a problem and probably the commonest of these is where a path across a field has been ploughed up. It is legal for a farmer to plough up a path provided that he restores it within two weeks, barring exceptionally bad weather. This does not always happen and here the walker is presented with a dilemma. Does he follow the line of the path, even if this inevitably means treading on crops, or does he use his common sense and walk around the edge of the field? The latter course of action often seems the best but, as this means that you would be trespassing, you are, in law, supposed to keep to the exact line of the path, avoiding unnecessary damage to crops. In the case of other obstructions which may block a path (illegal fences and locked gates etc.), common sense again has to be used in order to negotiate them by the easiest method (detour or removal). If you have any problems negotiating rights of way, you should report the matter to the Rights of Way Department of the relevant county, borough or metropolitan district council. They will then take action with the landowner concerned.

Apart from rights of way enshrined by law, there are a number of other paths available to walkers. Permissive or concessionary paths have been created where a landowner has given permission for the public to use a particular route across his land. The main problem with these is that, as they have been granted as a concession, there is no legal

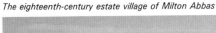

The eighteenth-century estate village of Milton Abbas

right to use them and therefore they can be extinguished at any time. In practice, many of these concessionary routes have been established on land owned either by large public bodies such as the Forestry Commission, or by a private one, such as the National Trust, and as these mainly encourage walkers to use their paths, they are unlikely to be closed unless a change of ownership occurs.

Walkers also have free access to Country Parks (except where requested to keep away from certain areas for ecological reasons, e.g. wildlife protection, woodland regeneration, safeguarding of rare plants etc.), canal towpaths and most beaches. By custom, though not by right, you are generally free to walk across the open and uncultivated higher land of mountain, moorland and fell, but this varies from area to area and from one season to another — grouse moors, for example, will be out of bounds during the breeding and shooting seasons and some open areas are used as Ministry of Defence firing ranges, for which reason access will be restricted. In some areas the situation has been clarified as a result of 'access agreements' between the landowners and either the county council or the National Park authority, which clearly define when and where you can walk over such open country.

Countryside Access Charter

Your rights of way are:
- Public footpaths — on foot only. Sometimes waymarked in yellow
- Bridleways — on foot, horseback and pedal cycle. Sometimes waymarked in blue
- Byways (usually old roads), most 'roads used as public paths' and, of course, public roads — all traffic has the right of way

Use maps, signs and waymarks to check rights of way. Ordnance Survey Pathfinder and Landranger maps show most public rights of way

On rights of way you can:
- take a pram, pushchair or wheelchair if practicable
- take a dog (on a lead or under close control)
- take a short route round an illegal obstruction or remove it sufficiently to get past

Some of the surviving woodlands of Cranborne Chase

You have a right to go for recreation to:
- public parks and open spaces — on foot
- most commons near older towns and cities — on foot and sometimes on horseback
- private land where the owner has a formal agreement with the local authority

In addition you can use the following by local or established custom or consent, but ask for advice if you are unsure:
- many areas of open country, such as moorland, fell and coastal areas, especially those in the care of the National Trust, and some commons
- some woods and forests, especially those owned by the Forestry Commission
- Country Parks and picnic sites
- most beaches
- canal towpaths
- some private paths and tracks

Consent sometimes extends to horse-riding and cycling

For your information:
- county councils and London boroughs maintain and record rights of way, and register commons
- obstructions, dangerous animals, harassment and misleading signs on rights of way are illegal and you should report them to the county council
- paths across fields can be ploughed, but must normally be reinstated within two weeks
- landowners can require you to leave land to which you have no right of access
- motor vehicles are normally permitted only on roads, byways and some 'roads used as public paths'

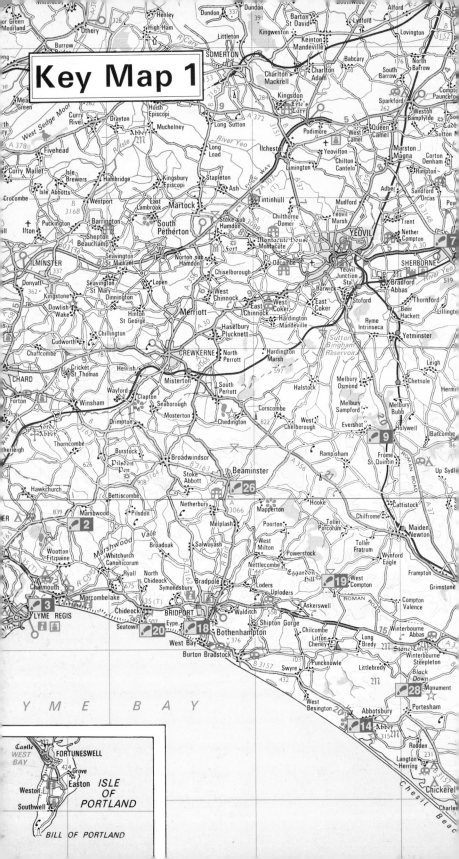

Key Map 1

Key Map 2

CONVENTIONAL SIGNS

1:25 000 or 2½ INCHES to 1 MILE

ROADS AND PATHS

Not necessarily rights of way

M I or A 6(M)	M I or A 6(M)	Motorway
A 31 (T)	A 31 (T)	Trunk road
A 35	A 35	Main road
B 3074	B 3074	Secondary road
A 35	A 35	Dual carriageway

Narrow roads with passing places are annotated

Road generally more than 4m wide

Road generally less than 4m wide

Other road, drive or track

Unfenced roads and tracks are shown by pecked lines

Path

RAILWAYS

Multiple track	Standard gauge
Single track	
	Narrow gauge
	Siding
	Cutting
	Embankment
	Tunnel
	Road over & under
	Level crossing; station

PUBLIC RIGHTS OF WAY

Public rights of way may not be evident on the ground

Public paths { Footpath / Bridleway

Byway open to all traffic
Road used as a public path

DANGER AREA
Firing and test ranges in the area
Danger!
Observe warning notices

The indication of a towpath in this book does not necessarily imply a public right of way
The representation of any other road, track or path is no evidence of the existence of a right of way

BOUNDARIES

— · — · — County (England and Wales)

— — — — District

⟶⟶⟶⟶⟶ London Borough

············· Civil Parish (England)* Community (Wales)

— — — — — Constituency (County, Borough, Burgh or European Assembly)

Coincident boundaries are shown by the first appropriate symbol

*For Ordnance Survey purposes County Boundary is deemed to be the limit of the parish structure whether or not a parish area adjoins

SYMBOLS

	Place	with tower	
	of	with spire, minaret or dome	
+	worship	without such additions	

Glasshouse; youth hostel

Bus or coach station

Lighthouse; lightship; beacon

Triangulation station

Triangulation point on { church or chapel / lighthouse, beacon / building; chimney

pylon pole Electricity transmission line

VILLA Roman antiquity (AD 43 to AD 420)

Castle Other antiquities

Site of antiquity

1066 Site of battle (with date)

Gravel pit

Sand pit

Chalk pit, clay pit or quarry

Refuse or slag heap

Sloping wall

Water	Mud

Sand; sand & shingle

National Park or Forest Park Boundary

NT National Trust open access

NT National Trust limited access

NTS NTS National Trust for Scotland

VEGETATION

Limits of vegetation are defined by positioning of the symbols but may be delineated also by pecks or dots

Coniferous trees

Non-coniferous trees

Coppice

Orchard

Scrub

Marsh, reeds, saltings

Bracken, rough grassland
In some areas bracken ( ) and rough grassland ( ) are shown separately

Heath

Shown collectively as rough grassland on some sheets

In some areas reeds ( ) and saltings ( ) are shown separately

HEIGHTS AND ROCK FEATURES

50 } Determined { ground survey
285 } by { air survey

Surface heights are to the nearest metre above mean sea level. Heights shown close to a triangulation pillar refer to the ground level height at the pillar and not necessarily the summit.

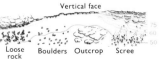

Vertical face

Loose rock Boulders Outcrop Scree

Contours are at 5 metres vertical interval

TOURIST INFORMATION

✝	Abbey, Cathedral, Priory		Garden	☆	Other tourist feature
	Aquarium		Golf course or links	✕	Picnic site
人	Camp site		Historic house		Preserved railway
	Caravan site		Information centre		Racecourse
	Castle		Motor racing		Skiing
	Cave		Museum		Viewpoint
	Country park	!	Nature or forest trail		Wildlife park
	Craft centre		Nature reserve		Zoo
P	Parking				
PC	Public Convenience (in rural areas)				

𝔐 Ancient Monuments and Historic Buildings in the care of the Secretary of State for the Environment which are open to the public.

Castle
SAILING   Selected places of interest

T   Public telephone

Mountain rescue post

National trail or Recreational Path Long Distance Route (Scotland only)

NATIONAL PARK   Boundary of National Park access land
ACCESS LAND   Private land for which the National Park Planning Board have negotiated public access

Pennine Way   Named path

◄   Access Point

WALKS

1	Start point of walk		Featured walk	➜	Route of walk
					Alternative route

ABBREVIATIONS   1:25 000 or 2½ INCHES to 1 MILE also 1:10 000/1:10 560 or 6 INCHES to 1 MILE

BP,BS	Boundary Post or Stone	P	Post Office	A,R	Telephone, AA or RAC
CH	Club House	Pol Sta	Police Station	TH	Town Hall
F V	Ferry Foot or Vehicle	PC	Public Convenience	Twr	Tower
FB	Foot Bridge	PH	Public House	W	Well
HO	House	Sch	School	Wd Pp	Wind Pump
MP,MS	Mile Post or Stone	Spr	Spring		
Mon	Monument	T	Telephone, public		

Abbreviations applicable only to 1:10 000/1:10 560 or 6 INCHES to 1 MILE

Ch	Church	GP	Guide Post	TCB	Telephone Call Box
F Sta	Fire Station	P	Pole or Post	TCP	Telephone Call Post
Fn	Fountain	S	Stone	Y	Youth Hostel

FOLLOW THE COUNTRY CODE
Enjoy the countryside and respect its life and work

Guard against all risk of fire	Take your litter home
Fasten all gates	Help to keep all water clean
Keep your dogs under close control	Protect wildlife, plants and trees
Keep to public paths across farmland	Take special care on country roads
Leave livestock, crops and machinery alone	Make no unnecessary noise
Use gates and stiles to cross fences, hedges and walls	

Reproduced by permission of the Countryside Commission

1 Hengistbury Head

Start:	Hengistbury Head
Distance:	3 miles (4.75 km)
Approximate time:	1½ hours
Parking:	Hengistbury Head
Refreshments:	Café at Hengistbury Head car park
Ordnance Survey maps:	Landranger 195 (Bournemouth & Purbeck) and Outdoor Leisure 22 (New Forest)

General description *Hengistbury Head is the prominent headland to the east of Bournemouth that overlooks Christchurch Harbour, the most easterly part of the Dorset coast. This area of heath, grass, scrub and saltmarsh, criss-crossed by well constructed and well maintained paths, provides excellent views and, despite its nearness to Bournemouth, preserves an appealing aura of wilderness, making it ideal for a short stroll.*

The walk starts at the café and information kiosk at the far end of the car park. Bear right along the gravel track (not the tarmac track) towards the Double Dykes, an Iron Age fortification comprising two ramparts and a ditch, built to defend the headland on its landward side. Do not go through the dykes but turn right beside the outer rampart towards the cliffs. Here turn left (**A**) and walk along another broad, gravel track, climbing up to the triangulation pillar on the highest point of Hengistbury Head. The multitude of tracks and paths can be a little confusing, but keep along the main track all the while and the route to the top of the headland is obvious. From here the magnificent all-round view takes in the Isle of Purbeck, Bournemouth, Christchurch Harbour, the Hampshire coast and the Isle of Wight.

Continue along the track, passing a coastguard look-out station and keeping to the top of the cliffs all the while, at one stage passing to the right of a pool, one of several that have been formed in the abandoned ironstone quarries on the headland. Near the end of the promontory, follow the track around to the left and ahead is a superb view over Christchurch Harbour, with the tower of Christchurch Priory standing out prominently. Descend steps to the beach, walk past some wooden chalets to join a tarmac drive and keep along it, passing to the right of a lagoon, to the southern shore of the harbour (**B**).

Turn left onto a sand and shingle path that runs along the edge of the water, keeping parallel to Hengistbury Head on the left.

Descending from Hengistbury Head to Christchurch Harbour

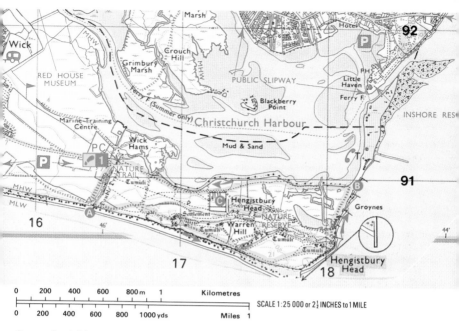

SCALE 1:25 000 or 2½ INCHES to 1 MILE

Cross a footbridge over an inlet and continue along the edge of the saltmarsh, looking out for a path that leads off to the left. Follow this path, initially narrow and overgrown between bushes and scrub, later across marshland and finally between trees, to rejoin the tarmac drive (**C**).

Turn right to return to the start, passing through the Double Dykes again to reach the café and information kiosk.   ☐

2 Lambert's Castle and Coney's Castle

Start:	National Trust car park at Lambert's Castle Hill
Distance:	3½ miles (5.5 km)
Approximate time:	2 hours
Parking:	Lambert's Castle Hill
Refreshments:	None
Ordnance Survey maps:	Landranger 193 (Taunton & Lyme Regis) and Pathfinder 1316, SY 29/39 (Lyme Regis & Axminster)

General description *This walk links two prehistoric forts, both now National Trust properties, which occupy adjacent hills above Marshwood Vale in west Dorset. Although only a short walk, it offers spectacular views over the vale to the encircling hills and towards Lyme Regis and the coast, an intimate patchwork of farmland and woodland that reveals the Dorset landscape at its finest.*

At the far end of the car park, just beyond a National Trust information board, climb a stile and follow a clear track across open grassland, parallel to the edge of woodland and a wire fence on the left. Go through a gap in the earthworks of the Iron Age fort that crowns Lambert's Castle Hill (839 feet (256 m)) to enter the fort (**A**) – an open, grassy area with the most magnificent all-round views, especially over the Marshwood Vale and looking towards the coast.

Turn right and follow the track southwards through the fort, passing a half-hidden triangulation pillar. There are lots of paths and tracks across the grassland, but keep ahead steadily downhill, between bracken, gorse and widely scattered trees, along a straight stony track. Pass through a gate and continue down to a National Trust sign and

SCALE 1:25 000 or 2½ INCHES to 1 MILE

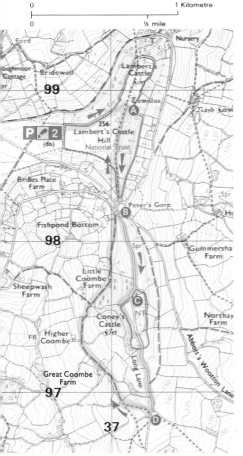

junction of lanes. Continue to another junction a few yards ahead (**B**) and keep straight on along the lane signposted to Wootton Fitzpaine, which curves up to the top of a hill. Soon after reaching the edge of woodland on the right, you arrive at the National Trust's Coney's Castle car park. The lane runs through this second Iron Age fort and both sides are worth exploring for a number of reasons: firstly because the ramparts themselves are of historic interest, secondly because they offer fine views in every direction over lush countryside, and thirdly because of the superb ancient trees that crown the hill.

The route continues along the lane for another 50 yards (46 m) past the car park. Where it curves to the left (by an entrance sign on the left), turn right (**C**) through a gap in an embankment, bear left through a gate and head straight across the open grassy area occupying the middle of the fort. To the right is the finest view of the walk, extending in a wide arc over well wooded hills to Lyme Regis and the coast. At the far end of this grassy ledge, head downhill onto a lower ledge and turn left to rejoin the lane. Turn right along it for another ¼ mile (0.5 km), heading downhill.

At the entrance to Great Coombe Farm, turn very sharply to the right (**D**) (almost doubling back) along a tarmac farm track that curves first to the left and later to the right to reach the farm. The track passes below the steep western edge of Coney's Castle Hill to the right and there is a fine view of the thickly wooded plateau of Wootton Hill to the left. Pass to the right of the farm, go through a metal gate and continue along a broad hedge-lined track, soon heading uphill. Go through another metal gate, keep along the left-hand edge of woodland and continue to a third metal gate. Pass through that and walk on to reach the junction of lanes that you crossed before (**B**).

Here you rejoin the outward route and retrace your steps to the start, enjoying more outstanding views. ☐

Looking over Marshwood Vale from Lambert's Castle Hill

3 Lyme Regis

Start:	Lyme Regis
Distance:	4 miles (6.5 km)
Approximate time:	2½ hours
Parking:	Lyme Regis
Refreshments:	Pubs, cafés and restaurants in Lyme Regis
Ordnance Survey maps:	Landranger 193 (Taunton & Lyme Regis) and Pathfinder 1316, SY 29/39 (Lyme Regis & Axminster)

General description *A spectacular view over Lyme Regis and the coast comes just after the start of the walk; the rest of the route explores the attractive and well wooded country of the Lim valley behind Lyme Regis. The return to the town and coast is along the riverbank, making a relaxing and pleasant finale to a highly enjoyable walk.*

Lyme Regis is a most delightful holiday resort. A bustling main street leads down towards the harbour, a row of charming seventeenth- and eighteenth-century cottages overlooks the sea, and a maze of narrow streets winds through the old part of the town by the little River Lim. At one time it was an important port and centre for woollen and boat-building industries, its prosperity

Lyme Regis harbour

largely created by the construction of the Cobb, a curving stone wall protecting both town and harbour that has become the symbol of Lyme Regis. In 1685 the Duke of Monmouth, illegitimate son of Charles II, landed here to drive his uncle James II from the throne, an attempt that ended in disaster at the Battle of Sedgemoor and in the duke's subsequent death.

Following its decline as a port, Lyme Regis became a fashionable seaside resort, made popular by both Pitt the Elder and the Younger and later patronised by a series of writers, including Henry Fielding, Jane Austen and Lord Tennyson. Nowadays its many hotels and guest-houses, shops and inns, restaurants and tearooms testify to its continued popularity.

The walk starts at the bottom end of Broad Street. Facing the sea, turn left and cross Buddle Bridge over the River Lim. Walk past the nineteenth-century guildhall and museum and turn left uphill, passing to the left of the church, an interesting but confusing building. This is because a mainly early-sixteenth-century building was grafted onto an existing twelfth-century church. The western part of the church was the original Norman nave.

Soon after passing a car park, turn right (**A**) over a stile by a footpath signposted 'Coast Path, Charmouth', and head diagonally across a field. Bear right to climb a stile near the top corner — you will see a superb view from here over the town — and continue steadily uphill across the next field to a kissing-gate. Pass through this and keep ahead across the next field to go through another kissing-gate and at a 'Coast Path' sign turn left along a track running between a hedge on the left and woodland on the right.

Pass beside a barrier and turn right along a wide uphill lane. Just after passing to the left of a golf-course you reach a junction (**B**); turn sharp left along the main road and after 200 yards (183 m) bear right through a waymarked gate to follow a broad downhill track to the right of some trees. Ahead are pleasant views over the well wooded Lim valley. Go through a gate, continue downhill into the valley and at a T-junction of tracks turn right (**C**). Go through another gate and keep ahead along a tree-lined track, heading down to pass to the right of a house.

Bear left around the end of the house and then turn right to a pair of gates. Turn left to go through the left-hand one of these and head straight across the middle of a field, passing through an obvious gap in a hedge and keeping in the same direction downhill across the rough field ahead. Make for the far end of the field at a point about 100 yards (91 m) to the right of its left-hand edge and border with Sleech Wood. Here you have to search for an almost-hidden footbridge over a stream — there is a path between bushes that leads down to it but it is difficult to spot. Cross the footbridge, briefly entering Devon, and head uphill across a field towards a farmhouse, making for a stile in a fence to the left of the house. Do not climb this stile but turn left and, keeping by a wire fence on the right, climb another stile by a public footpath sign.

Now continue in a straight line across a large, sloping field, from which there are good views of the valley ahead and the densely wooded slopes of Sleech Wood to the left. A line of telegraph poles acts as a useful waymark. At the far end of the field go through a gate into the wood, follow the straight path ahead through it, and then continue along a delightful grassy, hedge-lined path which, after passing to the right of a farm, curves to the right to emerge onto a lane. Turn left along the lane between houses for about 100 yards (91 m) to where it bears right and, at a public bridleway sign, keep straight ahead (**D**) along a concrete track. In a short while the track bears right to continue along the edge of Sleech Wood, keeping by a

stream on the left. This is a most attractive part of the walk.

By a picturesque old thatched mill building, keep ahead by the stream, ignoring a footbridge on the left and passing to the left of the mill. Go through a waymarked gate, head across a grassy area to climb a footbridge over the River Lim (re-entering Dorset), and turn left (**E**) to walk across a delightful riverside meadow, parallel to the river on the left. Climb a stile or go through a metal kissing-gate at the far end of the meadow and walk along the narrow path ahead to cross the river.

Continue along the left bank of the river, soon joining a broad track that takes you as far as Horn Bridge on the edge of Lyme Regis. Cross a road and continue along the lane ahead (Windsor Terrace). Keeping by the river, cross several roads before again crossing the river to walk along its right bank, continuing along an attractive street of old and new cottages and houses to rejoin the river. Finally take the riverside walk, passing to the left of the Leper's Well set in a pleasant public garden; there was a leper hospital near here in the Middle Ages. At a T-junction, turn right back to the town centre and start. □

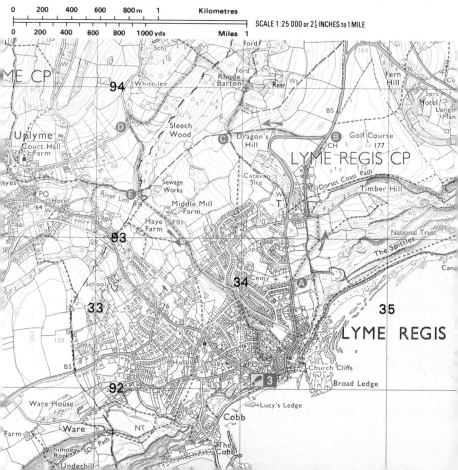

4 Sturminster Newton and the River Stour

Start:	Sturminster Newton
Distance:	4 ½ miles (7.25 km)
Approximate time:	2 ½ hours
Parking:	Sturminster Newton
Refreshments:	Pubs and cafés at Sturminster Newton, pub at Fiddleford
Ordnance Survey maps:	Landranger 194 (Dorchester & Weymouth), Pathfinders 1280, ST 61/71 (Sherborne & Sturminster Newton) and 1281, ST 81/91 (Shillingstone & Tollard Royal)

General description *Much of this easy walk in the gentle countryside of the Stour valley appears to be through a landscape where time has stood still, reflecting a more relaxed and unhurried bygone age. The ingredients that help to create this atmosphere are: an old market town with connections with Thomas Hardy, delightful undisturbed meadows where you still walk through wildflowers, attractive broadleaved woodland, two picturesque mills, an impressive seventeenth-century bridge and pleasant views over the gently meandering river across Blackmoor Vale.*

The sleepy and unspoilt market town of Sturminster Newton, a harmonious mixture of old and new, of stone, brick and thatch, lies on the edge of Blackmoor Vale above a bend in the River Stour and retains a pleasantly old-fashioned air. The church or minster from which it gets its name is an imposing building, mostly rebuilt in the nineteenth century but retaining its fine fifteenth-century tower.

The walk begins in the Market Place by the base of the fifteenth-century market cross. Just beyond the cross, turn left at a 'To the Church' notice, and after a few yards turn right along a lane that later bends to the left to reach the church. Walk through the churchyard, keeping to the left of the church, and at a T-junction of paths turn left between houses to a lane. Turn right and, in front of a large house (just before the lane curves to the right), turn left along a hedge-lined track.

Climb a waymarked stile and then bear slightly right (**A**) to follow a well worn and distinct grassy path across delightful riverside meadows, full of buttercups in summertime. To the right are pleasant views of the gently rolling and well wooded hills on the other side of the River Stour. Climb a stile and continue across the meadowland to where it narrows almost to a point; here turn left over a footbridge and bear right to climb a stile. Keep ahead to cross another footbridge over the river and continue to Fiddleford Mill, a former corn mill and the first of two mills passed on this walk. Turn right by the mill buildings to continue along a tarmac lane, passing Fiddleford Manor, a most attractive building dating back to the fourteenth century.

Keep ahead to where the lane bends to the right (**B**) and continue along it, passing the Fiddleford Inn, to the main road. Turn right and, just after crossing a bridge over the stream, turn left (**C**) at a footpath sign to climb a stile beside a metal gate. Walk gently uphill, keeping by a wire fence and hedge on the right, climb two stiles and continue along the right-hand edge of the next field, now with woodland on the right. Soon after passing over the brow of the hill and before reaching the field corner, turn right over a

Sturminster Newton Mill by the River Stour

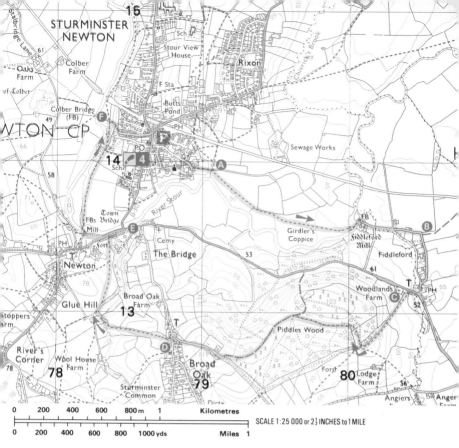

stile to enter Piddles Wood, and follow a track through this lovely woodland of well spaced trees and open glades. At a fork, take the left-hand track, continue more or less in a straight line to a T-junction, and turn left to follow a track to a lane.

Turn right downhill along the lane into the hamlet of Broad Oak, and at a T-junction cross the road and turn slightly left (**D**) along a track that leads to a waymarked kissing-gate. Go through and turn half-right to follow an indistinct path across a meadow, soon joining and keeping by a hedge on the right. Head gently downhill, go through a kissing-gate and continue between trees down to a footbridge. Cross it, head uphill to a lane and immediately turn sharp right onto a narrow, hedge-lined path. Follow this path to a stile on the edge of a field, climb it and keep in the same direction (no visible path) across the corner of this large field, making for a metal gate in front of you. The ruined building seen ahead is a medieval house on the site of an ancient earthwork.

Go through the metal gate, keep ahead across rough pasture to reach and negotiate a strange half-stile and half-gate, go through another gate a few yards ahead, and continue along the right-hand edge of the pasture with a wire fence on the right. Climb a stile and head down steps, turning sharp

right down to the road opposite Town Bridge, a fine seventeenth-century structure (**E**).

Turn sharp left along the road, keeping the river on the right and taking the first turning on the right down to Sturminster Newton Mill. This picturesque building in a lovely position beside the River Stour, a working flour mill again after being restored, dates from the seventeenth and eighteenth centuries. Turn right around the side of the mill, cross a footbridge, turn right again over another footbridge, and turn left to go through a kissing-gate. Now follow a most attractive grassy path across more riverside meadows, go through a kissing-gate, and continue along the left-hand edge of a recreation ground to go through another kissing-gate to the left of a large house. Thomas Hardy lived in this house for two years (1876–8), during which time he wrote *The Return of the Native*.

Continue past the house – ahead is a lovely view over the gently meandering Stour across Blackmoor Vale – descending gently and bearing slightly right to climb a stile. Turn right (**F**) and head uphill by a hedge and wire fence on the right, bearing right to a metal kissing-gate. Go through it onto a tarmac drive and follow this back to the centre of Sturminster Newton. □

5 Tyneham and Worbarrow Bay

Start:	Tyneham
Distance:	3½ miles (5.5 km)
Approximate time:	2 hours
Parking:	Tyneham
Refreshments:	None
Ordnance Survey maps:	Landranger 194 (Dorchester & Weymouth) and Outdoor Leisure 15 (Purbeck)

General description This walk is entirely within the Lulworth Army Ranges, a large area of land (over 7,000 acres) used for firing and tank-training mostly since the Second World War. Paradoxically this long period of army occupation has had more beneficial than harmful effects on the landscape, preserving the flora and fauna from modern intensive farming practices and protecting the coastline from intrusive commercial development. The one disadvantage is that the ranges are not always open and there is restricted access. Waymarking is excellent, the route is easy to follow but, as the frequent warning notices tell you, it is essential to use only the permitted paths and tracks and always to keep within the line of regular yellow-topped posts because of the danger of unexploded shells. This will enable you to enjoy a most scenic and fascinating walk through a landscape that has remained largely unchanged for half a century.

The range walks are usually open at weekends, on bank holidays and throughout the summer, but for details consult local tourist information offices.

Tyneham is a ghost village, deserted since 1943 when the War Office took over the surrounding area, initially as a training ground for Allied troops preparing for the D-day Normandy landings. The Victorian church, schoolroom and other abandoned and partially-ruined buildings give it a movingly melancholy air, while at the same time making it a place of great historic curiosity. This curiosity can be satisfied in the church, where an exhibition tells the history of this unusual museum piece.

Start by facing the church and turn right

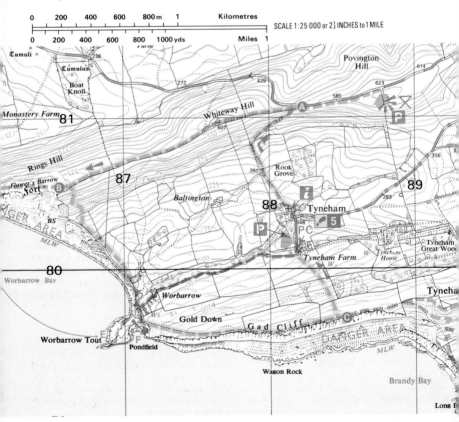

The abandoned and ruined village of Tyneham

over a stile to take the uphill track that passes to the right of the church. The track climbs steadily and bears right to reach the top of the ridge. Do not continue onto the road but turn left (**A**), climb a stile, and follow another track gently uphill over Whiteway Hill, in spring a most colourful combination of bluebells and vivid yellow gorse. There are fine views to the left, at first over the Tyneham valley and later of the coast, and to the right, over heathland (somewhat disfigured by tank tracks) with East Lulworth church and Lulworth Castle in the distance.

Continue past a triangulation pillar and, where the track bears right to head downhill, keep ahead to climb a stile and continue through the outer defences of the Iron Age fort of Flower's Barrow. In the middle of the fort, a footpath sign directs you to the left (**B**); pass through the outer earthworks again to a stile and ahead is a magnificent view over Worbarrow Bay. Climb the stile and head

steeply downhill towards the sea, climb another stile and continue along a fence on the right. To the right are spectacular views of the switchback cliffs stretching away to Lulworth Cove and beyond. Climb a stile to descend to the beach, passing the ruins of former fishermen's cottages.

Cross a plank over a stream, turn left onto an uphill track and after a few yards turn right up some steps to a flat, grassy area. Continue to a stile, climb it, and head steeply uphill along the edge of Gad Cliff. This is the most strenuous part of the walk but gives fine views over the Tyneham valley to the left and the coast to the right.

Shortly after climbing a stile, turn left (**C**) at a footpath marker-stone onto a wide, grassy path that heads quite steeply downhill towards Tyneham. At the bottom of the hill, the path bears left across a field, later bearing right to a stile. Climb it and keep ahead between trees to return to the village. □

6 Swanage and Durlston Head

Start:	Swanage
Distance:	4 miles (6.5 km)
Approximate time:	2 hours
Parking:	Swanage
Refreshments:	Pubs and cafés at Swanage, café at Durlston Country Park
Ordnance Survey maps:	Landranger 195 (Bournemouth & Purbeck) and Outdoor Leisure 15 (Purbeck)

General description *Fine coastal scenery is combined with constant reminders of Swanage's past as an important quarrying and stone-exporting centre. Indeed, the first half of the walk follows a well waymarked 'Victorian Trail' from the town to Durlston Head, passing through Durlston Country Park, the creation of a wealthy nineteenth-century industrialist. Soon after rounding Durlston Head, you return to Swanage by an inland route, enjoying superb views of the Purbeck ridge ahead.*

Swanage has been a popular seaside resort since Victorian times, but in the nineteenth century its prosperity was mainly based on the shipping of stone from the local quarries to London, where Purbeck stone was much in demand. Two men who made a fortune from this trade, John Mowlem and his nephew, George Burt, brought back various structures and parts of demolished buildings from the capital and used them to adorn the town. These include the clock tower near the pier, which originally stood near London Bridge, and the elaborate seventeenth-century façade of the otherwise late-nineteenth-century town hall, which came from the Mercers' Hall. On the quayside there

are the remains of tram-lines that were used to transport the stone to the pier, where it was loaded onto barges.

The walk begins by the entrance to the pier on the south side of the town, and the first part of it is not only along the coast path but also follows a 'Victorian Trail' (purple waymarks with Queen Victoria's head) that illustrates many features of the life and work of Mowlem and Burt, who had such an impact on the history and physical appearance of Swanage and the surrounding area.

To the right of the pier entrance, take the uphill road which soon becomes a rough track. Bear slightly right, in the direction of a footpath sign 'Downs and Coast Path', and continue through a car park and along a road.

Bear right to follow a broad, clear track onto the headland of Peveril Point, turn sharp right at the cliff edge (**A**), climb some steps, and continue across the grassy area on the cliff top. To the left are fine views over Durlston Bay to Durlston Head, and to the right you look across Swanage Bay to Ballard Down and the Old Harry Rocks. At the end of the grassy area, keep ahead to pass through a gate onto a road, turn left and, just after a right-hand bend, turn left again to descend steps at a 'Coast Path' footpath sign, here entering Durlston Country Park. Continue along a track through attractive cliff-top woodlands — both the tracks and the woods were the creation of George Burt. There are plenty of seats from which to enjoy the sea views. When you see a 'Victorian Trail' waymark leading to the right, keep ahead, following directions to 'Castle and Globe', to reach the nineteenth-century Durlston Castle, the focal point of Burt's estate and a typical example of a wealthy Victorian industrialist's fantasy of the Middle Ages. Nowadays it is used as a restaurant for visitors to the country park.

In front of the castle, bear left downhill (**B**) ('Coast Path' sign) along a track that curves to the right around Durlston Head, passing

Swanage from Peveril Point

the Great Globe on the right. This illustrates another of Burt's fantasies: his fascination with the natural world of sun, stars and oceans. It was placed here below his castle in 1887 and made out of Portland stone. Continue above Tilly Whim Caves, limestone quarries in which John Mowlem worked as a young boy, before going to London to make his fortune and build up the company that George Burt inherited.

Descend and then ascend to reach the lighthouse at Anvil Point, from which there is a fine view ahead along the coast to St Aldhelm's Head, and at the lighthouse turn right along a tarmac drive (**C**). Just after the drive bends sharply to the right (at the point where the white enclosing walls end), keep ahead quite steeply uphill across grass, and on reaching a well defined grassy track at the top, turn left onto it. Keep along it, parallel to a wall on the right, to reach a kissing-gate. Go through and turn right (**D**) either to climb a stone stile or to go through a gate.

Now follow a path along the right-hand edge of Round Down by a wall and embankment on the right, climb a stone stile, and continue along the straight, clear, undulating path ahead, following it over a series of stiles back to Swanage. Ahead are fine views of Ballard Down and the Purbeck ridge, and to the right you look across the town and Swanage Bay. The uneven ground to the left indicates former quarry workings.

Finally, keep along a downhill tarmac track past houses into the town and continue to a main road. Turn right and keep ahead to return to the town centre. A short detour, taking the first turning on the left, brings you to the Mill Pond, the most photographed part of Swanage, where the combination of the church and old cottages grouped around the pond makes an idyllic scene. The church is mostly Victorian but has a fourteenth-century tower.

In the town centre, bear right to return to the pier entrance. □

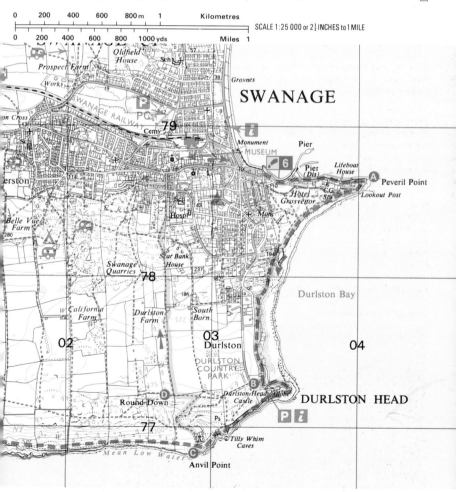

SCALE 1:25 000 or 2½ INCHES to 1 MILE

7 Sherborne Park

Start:	Sherborne
Distance:	5 ½ miles (8.75 km)
Approximate time:	2 ½ hours
Parking:	Sherborne
Refreshments:	Pubs and cafés at Sherborne
Ordnance Survey maps:	Landranger 183 (Yeovil & Frome) and Pathfinder 1280, ST 61/71 (Sherborne & Sturminster Newton)

General description *Sherborne Park was designed in the eighteenth century by 'Capability' Brown, the best known of landscape gardeners, and possesses all the ingredients that make up typical English landscaped parkland: a highly attractive mixture of grassland and farmland interspersed with areas of woodland, a deer park in which deer still roam, and a lake. Towards the end of this easy walk come fine views across the lake of both the ruined medieval castle and its successor. Leave plenty of time for a thorough exploration of Sherborne, one of the most delightful old towns in the country.*

Warm, golden-coloured stone buildings, dating from between the fifteenth and eighteenth centuries, line the narrow streets of Sherborne. Its principal building is the abbey, founded in 988 and at one time the seat of a bishop. The church is mainly fifteenth century and is a superb example of Perpendicular architecture, especially noted for the magnificent fan-vaulted roof in both nave and choir. The buildings of Sherborne School immediately to the north incorporate the cloisters and former domestic buildings of the abbey. Just to the east is the well preserved Abbey Conduit, the *lavatorium* or washing place of the monks, that formerly stood in the cloisters.

Sherborne boasts two castles lying on the eastern edge of the town. The ruins of the Old Castle date from the twelfth century and were given by a grateful Elizabeth I to Sir Walter Raleigh in 1592. He began the construction of the nearby New Castle, enlarged by its later owners, the Digby family, in the seventeenth century.

The walk starts in the centre of Sherborne at the Abbey Conduit. Walk down Long Street, a most attractive street of old houses, and continue along Oborne Road. At a restriction sign for large vehicles, turn left (**A**) by some riding stables, bear right uphill along a concrete track and keep ahead to go through the right-hand one of two metal gates, by a storage tank. Walk along the left-hand edge of a field, by a hedge on the left. To the right is a pleasant view over the well wooded landscape of the park, with the ruins of Sherborne Old Castle standing out prominently. Go through another metal gate, continue along an enclosed track, climb a stile, and keep ahead along a narrower path to a road.

Turn right along this busy main road — there is a footpath — for ½ mile (0.75 km), and just past St Cuthbert's Church at Oborne (all that remains is the sixteenth-century chancel), turn right (**B**) through a gate beside a cottage, at a footpath sign to Goathill and Haydon. Walk across the grass, climb a stile beside a wall, and keep ahead to pass through a metal gate and under a railway bridge to another metal gate. Go through it and bear left across a field (no visible path) to climb a stile near the far corner. Cross a plank over a ditch, climb another stile, and follow a clear path across the middle of a field. Go through a metal gate and continue across the middle of the next field to climb a stile into Crackmore Wood. From the stile the New Castle, Old Castle and tower of Sherborne Abbey can all be seen to the right.

After climbing the stile, keep ahead for a few yards and then turn right to follow an overgrown and rather indistinct path through the wood, keeping roughly in a straight line and parallel to the edge of the wood to the right, to reach a track. Turn left along it and bear right to a tarmac drive by the fine gateway to Sherborne Park. Turn right through the gateway and walk along the drive, which soon becomes a rough track, and take the first turning on the left. Go through a metal gate and continue along what is now a concrete track, turning right over a stile just in front of a house (**C**). Walk across the grass to join and keep by a wire fence on the left, cross a footbridge over the River Yeo, and continue along the left-hand

edge of a field, by an iron fence on the left. Go through a kissing-gate in a wall and follow a reasonably clear uphill grassy path through bracken, keeping more or less in a straight line. This is a lovely section of the walk through the deer park, which possesses some impressive ancient trees. At the top of the rise go through a kissing-gate and keep ahead through trees, by a wire fence on the left, to reach a track (**D**).

Turn right along the track to a tarmac drive, turn left for a few yards, and then turn right. Just before reaching some barns, turn left and right to pass behind the barns and continue along a straight track through conifer woodland. The track bends to the right, passing the remains of a wartime camp, and then bends to the left to a kissing-gate. Go through and continue along a pleasant track between bracken, heading downhill to go through a kissing-gate to the right of a thatched lodge cottage. Walk along a track, by a high wire fence on the right, go through yet another metal kissing-gate, and keep ahead. From here there are superb views to the right of the New Castle, lake and Old Castle, landscaped parkland at its finest.

At a junction of tracks bear right across grass to go through a metal kissing-gate, then follow a path across a field, heading up

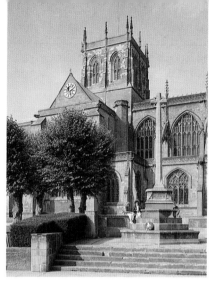

Sherborne Abbey

to another metal kissing-gate. Go through that and keep ahead, gradually descending to a road. Now comes a fine view of the town and abbey. Go through a metal kissing-gate onto the road (**E**), cross it, and take the road opposite, which leads over a level-crossing and the River Yeo back to the centre of Sherborne. □

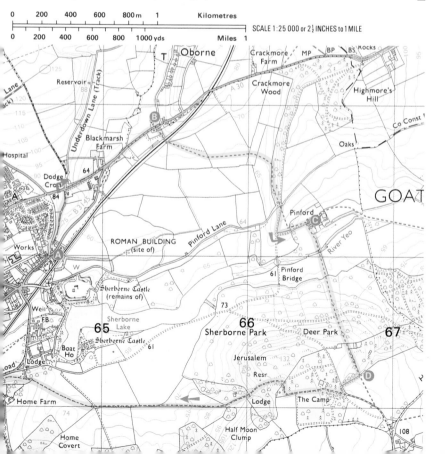

8 Bere Regis and Turners Puddle

Start:	Bere Regis
Distance:	5 miles (8 km)
Approximate time:	2½ hours
Parking:	Bere Regis
Refreshments:	Pubs at Bere Regis
Ordnance Survey maps:	Landranger 194 (Dorchester & Weymouth) and Outdoor Leisure 15 (Purbeck)

General description *Much of this walk is over the sandy heathland of Black Hill and Damer Hill, a splendid and largely unspoilt remnant of the once-extensive Egdon Heath that sprawled over much of eastern Dorset, reaching as far as Poole and Bournemouth. The views from the higher points, over Bere Regis and open downland to the north and the valley of the River Piddle or Trent and the conifers of Wareham Forest to the south, are superb.*

Bere Regis is dominated by the fifteenth-century flint and stone tower of its large parish church, a reflection of the village's former importance. The church was begun in the eleventh century but was enlarged over the following centuries. The interior is particularly noted for the elaborately carved and painted timber roof, which was a gift in 1475 from Cardinal Morton, a native of the village who, in Henry VII's reign, became Archbishop of Canterbury and Lord Chancellor of England, the most powerful man in the country. Among the carvings are full-sized figures of the twelve apostles. Also in the church are the tombs of the Turbervilles, the family that inspired Hardy's *Tess of the d'Urbervilles.*

Start in the car park by the church and turn right at a sign to the church, then turning left into the churchyard. Pass to the right of the church, go through a gate at the far end of the churchyard onto a road, and turn right.

Cross a stream — to the right are watercress beds — and turn right along Southbrook (**A**). Follow the road around a left-hand bend and, after a few yards where the road bends to the right, keep ahead along a gently ascending, sunken, hedge- and tree-lined path to the right of a cemetery. On reaching an attractive wooded area of fine oaks, turn half-right. Follow the indispensable blue waymarks painted on trees, heading uphill and bearing at first slightly to the right and then slightly to the left to follow a well defined path across an area of gorse-

and bracken-covered heathland.

Keep ahead at the first crossroads of paths (**B**), with grand views over the Piddle valley and Wareham Forest in front of you, and, just before the second crossroads, pass to the right of a standing stone known as the Devil's Stone. The next part of the walk is particularly attractive as you continue ahead downhill into the valley — a lovely mixture of gorse, bracken, fine old trees and grassy glades. Go through a gate and bear left, passing to the left of a farm, to reach a track in the valley bottom (**C**). Turn right along this broad track by a bridleway sign to Moor Lane, with the River Piddle on the left, to pass through the hamlet of Turners Puddle, now almost deserted and with its medieval church abandoned and derelict.

Continue through the pleasant broad valley for nearly ½ mile (0.75 km). Then where the track bears gently to the left, turn right through a metal gate (**D**). Follow a gently ascending track by a wire fence along the right-hand edge of a field, go through a metal gate, and, where the track divides, follow the direction of a blue waymark to take the left-hand fork. Soon you enter the conifers of Kite Hill Plantation, continuing along a clear track through the trees and bearing slightly right. The track curves first to the left and then briefly to the right before keeping more or less in a straight line through Piddle Wood, an attractive area of mixed woodland with some fine views through the trees on the left over bare and open country.

Where the track bears left to head downhill, bear right at a bridlepath sign to go through a gate and continue across the corner of a field, keeping roughly parallel to the edge of the wood on the left. Go through a metal gate, turn right (**E**), passing in front of farm buildings, go through another metal gate and continue along a broad track. At a crossroads of tracks, keep ahead along this splendid ridge-top track — gorse-lined and with fine views on both sides. Take the left-hand track at a fork and continue through bracken, trees and gorse, curving right, left, and right again to reach a crossroads of tracks (**B**).

Do not turn left here to rejoin the outward route, but turn more sharply left along a path that heads downhill through bracken, gradually bearing to the right and later continuing between tree-lined embankments to a T-junction. Turn left along a track that soon bends to the right, and then turn right along a straight, broad track that heads directly towards the houses on the edge of Bere Regis. Turn right along a road (**F**), turn left in front of a group of thatched cottages, cross a stream, and continue past modern houses to the main road. Bear right to return to the village centre. ☐

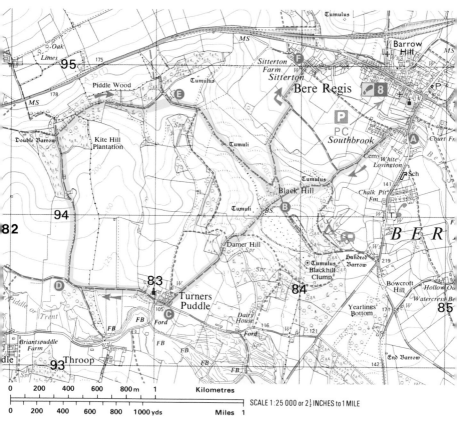

A remnant of Hardy's Egdon Heath on Damer Hill

9 Melbury Park

Start:	Evershot
Distance:	5½ miles (8.75 km). Shorter version 4½ miles (7.25 km)
Approximate time:	2½ hours (2 hours for shorter version)
Parking:	Roadside parking beside The Common at Evershot, a triangular green on the eastern edge of the village
Refreshments:	Pub at Evershot
Ordnance Survey maps:	Landranger 194 (Dorchester & Weymouth) and Pathfinder 1298, ST 40/50 (Crewkerne & Beaminster)

General description *From the attractive village of Evershot, at 700 feet (214 m) the second-highest village in Dorset, a tarmac drive leads northwards through Melbury Park, passing by Melbury House and Melbury Sampford church, to the equally attractive village of Melbury Osmond. The return leg uses quiet tracks and field paths, some of which may be muddy in parts. Except after prolonged dry weather, boots or wellingtons are recommended for this walk. The shorter version of the walk omits Melbury Osmond village.*

Thatched cottages lining the main street at Evershot and the old church at the far end of the village make a charming scene. The church, dating from the fifteenth century though largely rebuilt in the Victorian era, is unusual in that its short spire rises from one corner of the west tower instead of the centre.

The walk starts by The Common at the lower end of the village, where a public footpath sign to Melbury Osmond directs you along the tarmac drive through Melbury Park, soon passing a notice warning 'Private Road, No Vehicles, Footpath Only'. Keep ahead at a fork and the drive ascends gently to pass between stone gateposts. As you walk through the deer park, you pass some fine old trees and there are extensive views. At the next fork, keep ahead to pass through a tall, metal kissing-gate beside a cattle-grid, and then head gently downhill. Soon Melbury House can be glimpsed through the trees on the right and, after passing through another tall, metal kissing-gate, the drive curves to the right to reach the gates that lead up to the front of the house. Melbury House (not open to the public) was built by Sir Giles Strangways in the sixteenth century but enlarged and altered by successive members of the family over the following centuries. Beside it is the mainly fifteenth-century Melbury Sampford church, which contains many fine monuments.

In front of the house and church turn left (**A**) to continue along the straight tarmac drive through the park, passing through three more gates. Ahead is Melbury Osmond, the houses of the village climbing up the modest hill to the church, with dark trees in the background. After passing through the third gate, you leave the park to enter the village. At a T-junction by a thatched cottage, turn left (**B**) in order to do a loop round the village.

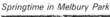
Springtime in Melbury Park

For the shorter version of the walk, turn right instead of left here and rejoin the full walk at (B) below.

The lane soon bears right and you cross a footbridge beside a ford to continue gently uphill between thatched cottages to the church. It was in Melbury Osmond church, heavily restored in the late nineteenth century, that Thomas Hardy's mother and father were married in 1849; his mother lived in a thatched cottage to the north of the church prior to her marriage.

Walk through the churchyard, passing in front of the church, onto a road, and turn right (C). Head gently downhill, cross a stream, and shortly afterwards turn right in front of a cottage along a straight concrete drive. After 50 yards (46 m), turn left over a stile, keep ahead across a field (no visible path) and, at the far end, turn right along the field edge, keeping parallel to a hedge on the left. At the bottom end, where the field narrows, bear slightly right to cross the stream again by a footbridge. Turn half-right across the next field (again no path), recrossing the concrete drive and making for a broad gap in the hedge in front. Go through this and continue across the next field, going through a gate to the left of a house. Walk along a track down to a T-junction, and turn left to rejoin briefly the previous route, having completed the loop around the village. Follow the lane around the left-hand bend and, where it bends sharply to the right (B), keep ahead.

The narrow, sunken, often muddy path between hedges and embankments leads to the one difficult part of the walk, where walking boots or wellingtons are likely to be needed. The soft and muddy path passes under a low bridge, where it may be quite deep in water after a rainy spell, and shortly afterwards you have to cross a stream without the benefit of a footbridge or stepping-stones.

Soon after crossing the stream, go through a gate into a field. From now on conditions under-foot greatly improve. Keep straight ahead to go through another gate and continue along a very pleasant, broad, green, hedge-lined track, with a narrow belt of trees on the right. Cross a road at a bend, keep along the wooded track ahead, go through a gate and continue, looking out for a public footpath sign that directs you through a gate on the right. Now turn left along the edge of a field, with a wire fence on the left, keeping parallel to the track that you have just left.

Pass through a gate to cross a stream, here picking up the track again, and continue to a T-junction by a public footpath sign. Turn left (D) along a broad track, passing to the right of Lucerne Lake, and continue through attractive mixed woodland to a junction of tracks. Turn right along a track that first heads steadily uphill, then descends gently between tree-lined embankments to a T-junction. Turn left to rejoin the tarmac drive through Melbury Park and retrace your steps to Evershot.   □

SCALE 1:25 000 or 2½ INCHES to 1 MILE

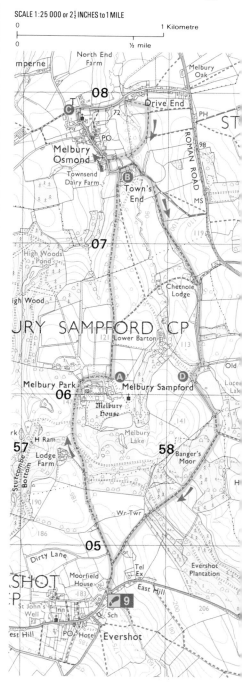

10 Lulworth Cove and Durdle Door

Start:	Lulworth Cove
Distance:	5 miles (8 km). Shorter version 4½ miles (7.25 km)
Approximate time:	2½ hours (2 hours for shorter version)
Parking:	Lulworth Cove
Refreshments:	Pubs and cafés at Lulworth Cove
Ordnance Survey maps:	Landranger 194 (Dorchester & Weymouth) and Outdoor Leisure 15 (Purbeck)

General description *The last mile of this walk is along what is unquestionably the most popular stretch of the Dorset coast, perhaps best avoided at bank holidays and other peak times. The reasons for its popularity are obvious: the exceptionally attractive and perfectly formed Lulworth Cove, the interesting geological phenomenon of Durdle Door, and the magnificent cliff scenery in between. In addition the walk explores some fine countryside immediately inland and provides an optional detour to the fascinating Fossil Forest, which is just inside the boundary of the Lulworth Army Ranges. (For information on access and the absolute need to observe the warning notices, see Walk 5.) Although only a short walk, it has several steep climbs.*

Lulworth Cove is almost perfectly circular, with just a narrow entrance to the south. It was formed by the sea breaching a weak point in the limestone cliffs and wearing away the softer rocks behind. In view of its seclusion and earlier remoteness, it is not surprising that it had a notorious reputation for smuggling during the eighteenth and nineteenth centuries.

Begin by facing the beach and, at a 'Coast Path and Youth Hostel' footpath sign, turn left up some steps. Climb a stile and keep ahead up more steps, climbing steeply onto the cliff top. The magnificent view over the cove more than repays the effort. The path follows the curve of the cove, heading downhill to a footpath sign (**A**).

*Turn left here for the shorter version of the walk if the Lulworth Army Ranges are closed and rejoin the full walk at (**A**) below.*

Turn right to continue steeply downhill to another footpath sign and turn left in the direction of Pepler Point and Fossil Forest. Passing to the left of the meagre remains of the thirteenth-century Little Bindon Chapel, thought to have been built on or near the site of the original Bindon Abbey (the monks later moved to Wool), go through a gate to enter the Lulworth Army Ranges. At a footpath marker-stone to Fossil Forest, turn right along a track to the cliff top (**B**). The Fossil Forest is below, reached by steps leading down to the beach. Here can be seen the petrified remains of tree stumps, fascinating fragments of a great forest that flourished in the age of the dinosaurs.

Retrace your steps past the chapel and on to where you turned right for the steep descent (**A**). Keep ahead steeply uphill

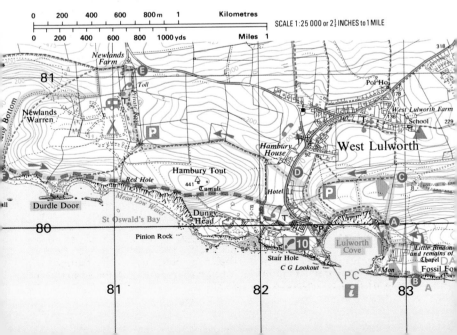

The natural arch of Durdle Door, one of the most popular spots on the Dorset coast

alongside the army ranges' fence on the right, following signs to West Lulworth youth hostel. Climb a stile and continue uphill to a footpath sign by another gate into the army ranges (**C**). Turn left, in the West Lulworth direction, along a wide, straight, grassy track above Lulworth Cove (more superb views), descending to meet a path. Turn right along it, by a wire fence bordering bushes on the left, and at a footpath sign turn left over a stile in the direction of Durdle Door. Follow a downhill path, between bushes on the left and a wire fence on the right, to a stile and onto a road.

Turn right along the road for about 50 yards (46 m) and, at a public footpath sign 'Coast Path and Durdle Door', turn left (**D**) down some steps, climb a stile, and walk along the left-hand edge of a field, by a wire fence on the left, to another stile. Climb that, go up some steps to climb yet another, and bear right along a track, signposted Durdle Door. To the right, the village and Victorian church of West Lulworth can be seen. The track keeps along the lower slopes of Hambury Tout. Climb a stile and continue, heading steadily uphill and climbing several more stiles to reach the edge of a caravan site. Turn right along a tarmac drive through the site and continue along a grassy, fenced path to the left of a road to reach a T-junction (**E**).

Turn left along the drive to Newlands Farm, turning right and then left to pass between the farm buildings. Continue along a track, and at a footpath sign to the interestingly named Scratchy Bottom, turn left through a metal gate. Head downhill along the left-hand edge of a field, by a wire fence on the left, towards the caravans again, following the field edge round to the right to a metal gate. Go through the gate and walk along the downhill track ahead, by a wire fence on the left. Pass through another metal gate and continue, now with a wire fence on the right, along a splendid, wide, grassy track, curving gradually to the left all the while through the beautiful, smooth-sided valley of Scratchy Bottom to reach the sea (**F**).

Climb a stile and a few yards ahead turn left to join the coast path. Head uphill and over the brow Durdle Door comes suddenly and spectacularly into view: one of the most visited and certainly the most photographed spot on the Dorest coast. The great natural archway in the limestone rock has been formed by the sea wearing away the softer clays that join the promontory to the main line of cliffs.

Continue along the coast path to Lulworth Cove, climbing several stiles and keeping close to the cliff edge all the while, enjoying the magnificent cliff scenery in both directions. After a stiff climb comes a superb view ahead of Lulworth Cove, the cliffs beyond it and the downs inland. Finally, descend a broad track to pass through the large car park to the beach and your starting point. □

11 Godlingston Heath and Ballard Down

Start:	Studland
Distance:	6 miles (9.5 km)
Approximate time:	3 hours
Parking:	National Trust South Beach car park at Studland
Refreshments:	Pub and café at Studland
Ordnance Survey maps:	Landranger 195 (Bournemouth & Purbeck) and Outdoor Leisure 15 (Purbeck)

General description *There is plenty of scenic variety on this walk, which includes the largest remaining area of open heathland in Dorset, the breezy chalk headland of Ballard Down flanked by Studland and Swanage Bays, and a fine coastal stretch that passes by the well known and distinctive Old Harry Rocks. Two other features of interest are the Agglestone Rock and the superb little Norman church at Studland. Much of the walk is on National Trust land.*

Studland church is one of the most perfect and complete Norman churches in the country, its low saddleback tower looking out over the sea. The interior is noted for the fine chancel arch, the magnificent vaulting in the chancel, and the interestingly grotesque carvings in the nave.

The walk starts at the National Trust South Beach car park. Turn left out of the car park and immediately left again to go through a gate and walk along a grassy path leading to the churchyard. Pass to the right of the Norman church and keep ahead to descend between hedge-banks to a road.

Turn right to a crossroads and continue along Heath Green Road as far as a public bridleway sign to Greenland, where you turn right (**A**) along a tree- and hedge-lined track. Go through a gate, continue along the right-hand edge of heathland, go through another gate, and bear right at a T-junction just ahead along a track between scrub and gorse. On reaching a broader track, turn left along it, pass between farmhouses and, by a bridleway stone to Agglestone Rock, follow the track through trees and over a footbridge, bearing left to emerge onto the open heathland of Godlingston Heath. Together with the adjacent Studland Heath, this makes up the largest surviving area of unspoilt heathland in Dorset, a fragment of the 'Great Heath' that once covered much of the eastern part of the county and so fascinated

Thomas Hardy. Nowadays much of it is a national nature reserve, home not only to many rare plants but also to all of Britain's reptiles, including adders.

Agglestone Rock can be seen on the ridge ahead just to the left. Make your way towards it, choosing one of the many sandy paths and tracks across the gorse, grass and heather. The huge rock, about 17 feet (5.2 m) high and weighing over 400 tons, is not only impressive in itself but makes a fine viewpoint, standing above the surrounding heath and overlooking coast and forest. From the rock the buildings of Poole and Bournemouth are clearly visible across Poole Harbour.

Continue past the rock, going through a wooden barrier and following a sandy track across the gently undulating heath to a junction by a National Trust footpath stone. Here veer slightly right, in the direction of Studland Road, continuing across the heath, which has a real feeling of wilderness despite the urban presence of Bournemouth on the horizon. This wilderness feeling is soon somewhat dispelled, however, by the sight of the well manicured greens of a golf-course, across which the next section of the walk proceeds. Follow the regular bridleway signs to Studland Road, keeping along the main track all the while and eventually going through a gate onto a road (**B**).

Cross over, climb the stile opposite and

keep in a straight line across another part of the golf-course, making for a direction-indicator ahead on the edge of trees. Continue downhill through the trees, climb a stile, bear right, and head across a field, descending to a stile near the bottom right-hand corner. Climb the stile onto a road, turn left onto a grassy path on the verge, and follow the road around a right-hand bend before turning right (**C**) along a track to a metal gate, where there is a National Trust sign for Ballard Down.

Go through the gate and walk along a grassy track, keeping by a wire fence on the left and climbing onto the down. After going through another gate, the track curves left to reach an obelisk on the top, which commemorates the local Water Board. In 1941 the obelisk was taken down so that it could not act as a landmark for enemy aircraft, but it was re-erected after the war. It is a magnificent viewpoint: looking to the left across Studland Bay and Poole Harbour to Bournemouth, to the right across Swanage and Swanage Bay to Peveril Point, and ahead towards the Isle of Wight.

Go through a gate and continue, passing through several gates and stiles, along a straight track across Ballard Down, the most easterly part of the Purbeck ridge: a superb ridge walk with the sea on three sides. After reaching a triangulation pillar, bear right and, in a few yards, bear left to join the coast path.

Agglestone Rock, a prominent landmark on Godlingston Heath

Follow the path as it curves left around Ballard Point and continues along the top of the grand chalk cliffs to the Old Harry Rocks. The nearer and bigger of the two rocks, with its natural arch, is Old Harry himself; the smaller is his wife, both of them (and the Pinnacles just to the south) formed by coastal erosion.

From the rocks follow the coast round to the left again (**D**) to continue along a broad straight track back to Studland. On the edge of the village, bear right at a footpath marker-stone to Studland, along another track that runs between wire fences, passing a wooden barrier and continuing downhill to a road. Turn right to return to the starting point. □

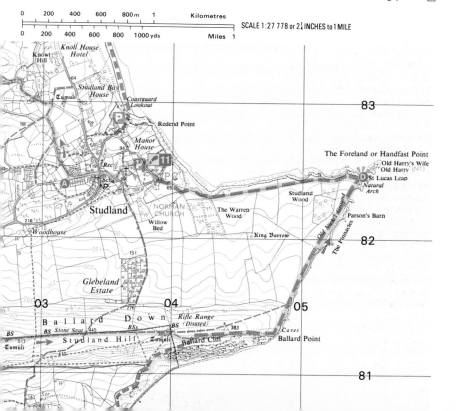

12 Bokerley Ditch and Pentridge Down

Start:	Large parking area at Bokerley Junction on A354, ½ mile (0.75 km) north of Woodyates
Distance:	5½ miles (8.75 km)
Approximate time:	3 hours
Parking:	Bokerley Junction
Refreshments:	None
Ordnance Survey maps:	Landranger 184 (Salisbury & The Plain) and Pathfinder 1282, SU 01/11 (Fordingbridge))

General description The first part of the walk is across the unploughed chalk pastureland of Martin Down, following the edge of Bokerley Ditch, an impressive fourth-century defensive earthwork that now forms part of the Dorset–Hampshire border. After leaving the ditch, you continue over the breezy ridge of Pentridge Down, before descending into the tiny, isolated hamlet of Pentridge and returning across fields to the start. The whole of this area is rich in both prehistoric and later remains and these, together with sweeping and extensive views across the Hampshire Downs, New Forest and Cranborne Chase, create a splendid and most absorbing walk.

From the parking area at Bokerley Junction, which is right on the boundary between Dorset and Hampshire, turn left along the road and look out for a blue-waymarked metal gate on the right. Go through it and bear left, keeping parallel to the road on the left and Bokerley Ditch on the right, following the ditch as it veers to the right. Bokerley Ditch is a well preserved, late Romano-British

earthwork that stretches for 4 miles (6.5 km) across the open downland of Cranborne Chase. It was built in the fourth century, probably to defend the lands of the Durotriges tribe from Saxon invaders, and is particularly impressive on the more vulnerable, eastern (Hampshire) side, where in places the rampart rises to over 20 feet (6 m).

You follow the eastern edge of the ditch for the next 1¾ miles (3 km) across Martin Down, a national nature reserve that is one of the largest remaining areas of natural, uncultivated chalk downland. Originally it would have enclosed the woodlands of Cranborne Chase on the right, but now the views on both sides, to the left looking across to the Hampshire Downs and to the right over the chase itself, are open and extensive. Ahead the ditch can be clearly traced, snaking across the country up to the ridge of Pentridge Down. The earthworks that can be seen to the left are much more recent, relics of army firing ranges and a vivid illustration of the continuity of military activity in the area.

Keep alongside the ditch all the while, passing to the left of a plantation and heading gently uphill towards the ridge. Just before reaching the trees that crown the ridge, turn right (**A**) by a nature reserve notice, along a broad chalky track that cuts first through the ditch itself and shortly afterwards through Grim's Ditch, clearly visible on the left. This is another earthwork, older than Bokerley Ditch and probably constructed in the Bronze Age. Also to the left is a Bronze Age burial mound.

Soon after entering woodland, turn very sharply to the right by a blue waymark, and in about 100 yards (91 m) turn left at another blue waymark to go through a gate. Follow the path ahead through woodland, by a wire fence on the right, until, on emerging from the trees, there is a grand view to the right with Bokerley Ditch dominating the middle of the scene. Continue, still by the wire fence on the right, soon passing the left-hand edge of a plantation. At this point, the official right of way bears left across the field to a group of

Bokerley Ditch, a Romano-British construction, runs for 4 miles (6.5 km) across open downland on the north-eastern borders of Dorset

trees on the ridge ahead, but if obstructed by crops, it is easier to continue to the end of the field and turn left to walk along the field edge, by a fence on the right, up to the trees. Keep ahead through the trees to go through a gate and continue, by a line of trees and wire fence on the left, along the ridge of Pentridge Down, enjoying the magnificent views on both sides: to the left over the New Forest and to the right over Cranborne Chase.

Make towards the prominent group of trees in front that crowns the summit of Penbury Knoll, occupied by a small Iron Age fort, and at the knoll turn right and head downhill through trees in the direction of the short, stumpy spire of Pentridge church. Continue across rough downland making for the bottom left-hand corner, where you climb a stile to follow a narrow, enclosed, overgrown downhill path to another stile. Climb that and bear slightly right downhill to climb a stile onto a lane.

Turn right into the small, sleepy and remote hamlet of Pentridge, taking the first turn on the left (**B**) to pass to the right of the attractive, restored medieval church, dedicated to the little-known Celtic saint, Rumbold. By the church, bear right at a fork and, in front of a cottage, go through a yellow-waymarked gate. Bear left to keep along the left-hand edge of a field, by a hedge on the left, and go through another gate onto a lane. Turn left for ¼ mile (0.5 km) and, where the lane bends to the left, turn sharp right along an enclosed grassy track (**C**). After about 200 yards (183 m), turn left along a much narrower enclosed path, later continuing first along the right- and later along the left-hand edge of fields, to reach a tarmac farm track by a house.

Turn left to the main road and turn right (**D**) along the road, using the wide verge, for just under ½ mile (0.75 km) to return to the start. □

13 Corfe Castle and the Purbeck ridge

Start:	Corfe Castle
Distance:	6 miles (9.5 km)
Approximate time:	3 hours
Parking:	Corfe Castle
Refreshments:	Pubs and cafés at Corfe Castle
Ordnance Survey maps:	Landranger 195 (Bournemouth & Purbeck) and Outdoor Leisure 15 (Purbeck)

General description *Soon after leaving Corfe Castle, you climb onto the Purbeck ridge for a most enjoyable ridge-top walk from which there are superb and extensive views: across to the coast on the left and over Wareham Forest and the Dorset heathlands on the right. After descending from the ridge and passing through the hamlet of East Creech, the route continues through a most attractive wooded area, before returning to Corfe Castle. Near the end comes a sudden and spectacular view of the dramatically sited castle ruins.*

Corfe Castle towers above the little grey-stone village, guarding the only gap in the Purbeck ridge. Its shattered walls and towers, occupying the steep slopes of a conical hill, make a splendid sight and reflect the stormy history of the castle. In the Saxon lodge that occupied the site, the boy-king Edward the Martyr was murdered on the orders of his scheming stepmother in 978. In the early thirteenth century, King John starved to death twenty-two French prisoners for supporting the claim to the throne of his nephew, Arthur of Brittany. During the Civil War between Charles I and Parliament, the castle was twice besieged by Parliamentary forces before the small garrison was forced to surrender in 1646. Shortly afterwards, the castle was slighted on Cromwell's orders. The existing ruins are mainly of the original Norman castle, dominated by the splendid keep, plus thirteenth-century extensions carried out by John and Edward I.

The highly picturesque village that grew up beneath the castle walls became the centre of the Purbeck stone and marble industry in the Middle Ages and there are many disused quarries nearby. Its church has a fine Perpendicular tower, but most of the rest of the building was rebuilt in the nineteenth century.

The walk starts in the centre of the village in front of the church. With your back to the church and facing the Greyhound Inn, take the lane to the left and in a few yards bear right, passing beside a yellow-waymarked barrier, along a downhill tarmac track, beside the little River Corfe on the left and below the castle walls on the right. On reaching a lane, turn left over a bridge and, after 50 yards (46 m), turn right over a stile (**A**). Now follow the direction of the blue, not the yellow, waymarking by turning left along a track that heads gently uphill across gorse-covered slopes with a wire fence on the left.

Where the track swings to the right by a

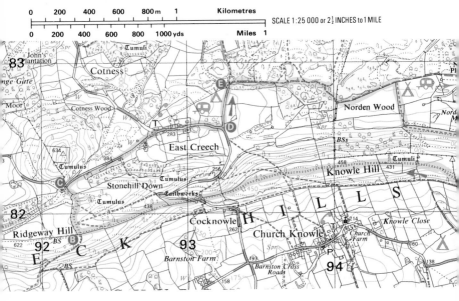

SCALE 1:25 000 or 2½ INCHES to 1 MILE

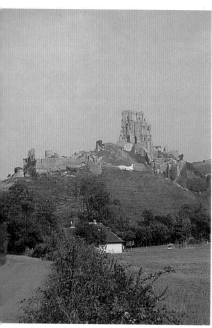

The dramatic ruins of Corfe Castle occupy the only gap in the Purbeck ridge

National Trust footpath marker-stone, keep ahead in the direction of Knowle Hill and Cocknowle to a gate. Go through and continue along a track to the next fork and National Trust marker-stone, where you take the right-hand uphill track, following directions to Ridge Path and Knowle Hill. Go through a metal gate and continue up to the top of the ridge, where you bear left to follow

the lovely, broad, grassy ridge over Knowle Hill. The little village that can be seen below on the left, clustered around its church, is Church Knowle. All the way along are superb views on both sides: the Purbeck coast to the left and Wareham Forest and part of Hardy's Egdon Heath to the right. Pass through two metal gates, continue past a commemorative stone, and descend to go through a metal gate onto a lane. To the right is a large quarry.

Keep ahead along the lane for 50 yards (46 m) and go through another metal gate to regain the ridge path that continues over Ridgeway Hill. Near the top you reach a junction of paths and tracks by a footpath marker-stone (**B**). Turn right along a downhill track, signposted to East Creech, go through a metal gate and at a fork bear right to continue to a lane (**C**). Turn right and follow the lane gently downhill into the hamlet of East Creech, little more than a farm and a few cottages, bearing right at a T-junction and passing the duck pond. At the next T-junction, turn left (**D**) along a lane signposted to Furzebrook, Stoborough and Wareham, and, where the lane bends to the left, turn right onto a blue-waymarked path to enter woodland (**E**).

Continue through the exceptionally beautiful Norden Wood, which was once a clay-mining area; the small pools that are scattered throughout the wood have been formed from old clay-pits and add to both the interest and the attractiveness of this part of the walk. Follow the blue waymarks all the time; at one stage you turn sharply to the right, after which the path meanders, eventually keeping along the right-hand edge of the wood. Look out for a stile on the right, climb it to leave the wood, and keep ahead along the right-hand edge of a field by a wire fence on the right, heading gently uphill towards the ridge. Climb a stile, go through a metal gate ahead, and continue across the next field to another metal gate near the top corner. Turn left, at first across bracken and later through trees and gorse, along a grassy path that runs across the lower slopes of the ridge, keeping by a wire fence on the left all the while.

Eventually you climb a stile to be confronted suddenly by an unexpected but most dramatic view of Corfe Castle. Keep ahead towards another stile but do not climb it; instead turn right (**F**) along a path with a wire fence on the left, passing below the slopes of gorse-covered West Hill. Continue gently downhill, passing to the right of a barn, to climb a stile onto a lane, here rejoining the outward route (**A**). Turn left, cross the bridge, and turn right to retrace your steps below the castle to the village centre.   □

14 Abbotsbury and Chesil Beach

Start:	Abbotsbury
Distance:	6 miles (9.5 km)
Approximate time:	3 hours
Parking:	Abbotsbury
Refreshments:	Pubs and cafés at Abbotsbury
Ordnance Survey maps:	Landranger 194 (Dorchester & Weymouth) and Pathfinder 1331, SY 58 (Abbotsbury)

General description *From Abbotsbury the route climbs up onto the open and windswept downs for a glorious scenic ridge walk of just over 1 mile (1.5 km) to the prehistoric fort of Abbotsbury Castle. Then follows a descent across fields to the coast and a walk beside the geological phenomenon of Chesil Beach back to Abbotsbury. Towards the end comes an optional diversion involving a climb to St Catherine's Chapel, well worth the effort not only for the architectural and historic appeal of the chapel, but also for the splendid view over Abbotsbury. Downland and coast, prehistoric fort and Chesil Beach, plus the various monastic associations of Abbotsbury – abbey remains, tithe barn, chapel and swannery – all create a fascinating and absorbing walk.*

Little remains of the former monastic greatness of Abbotsbury except for the fourteenth-century tithe barn, 270 feet (82 m) long and claimed to be the largest in the country, and St Catherine's Chapel on a hill above the village. Of the great Benedictine abbey itself, founded in the early eleventh century, there is not much to see apart from a gatehouse. As compensation there is the fine church, built mainly in the fifteenth and sixteenth centuries, immediately adjacent to the abbey. The village itself is a most attractive collection of warm-looking stone houses and cottages, many of them thatched, beautifully situated in a fold in the downs and about a mile (1.5 km) from the sea. One further monastic survival is the famous swannery to the south of the village, established by the monks in the fourteenth century.

Start in the village centre at the junction of Rodden Row, Church Street and Market Street. Walk along Market Street, take the first turning on the right (Back Street) and, after 200 yards (183 m), turn left along a track running between thatched cottages (**A**). Turn left at a fork and head gently uphill between hedge-banks on either side. The track turns sharply to the right and continues more steeply uphill, going through one metal gate and ahead to another one.

From this second gate there is a superb view behind of Abbotsbury village, church, tithe barn and St Catherine's Chapel on its hilltop. Go through the gate, keep ahead across a field, making for a gate and finger-post in a hedge corner. Go through this gate and bear slighly left, following signs to 'Hill Fort', to continue uphill along a grassy path between outcrops of rock. Keep in a straight line, heading towards another finger-post at the top of the ridge (**B**).

Here turn left to join the inland section of the Dorset Coast Path and keep alongside a wire fence on the right to a stile. Climb it and continue along this superb path that runs across the top of the broad, grassy ridge, with magnificent views to the left over the coast and to the right over rolling downland. You pass by several tumuli and climb a number of stiles – be careful at one stage to ignore a track that bears left to the road below – to reach a lane. Cross it and keep ahead at a footpath sign to West Bexington, climbing between gorse bushes and over a stile, then bearing slightly right to the earthworks of Abbotsbury Castle, a triangular Iron Age hill-fort commanding extensive views over downs and coast from its height of 710 feet (215 m). The path follows the line of the outer ramparts and eventually descends along a narrowing ridge before continuing over a grassy knoll, keeping parallel to the road on the left, to go through a gate in the far corner of a field to join the road (**C**).

Cross the road, climb a stile at a National Trust sign to Tulk's Hill, and continue by a wall on the left to where the wall ends at a finger-post. Here turn left, following directions to Chesil Beach, and head downhill along a grassy path between a wire fence and line of trees on the left and gorse and scrub on the right. A few yards after the end of the fence on the left, you reach another finger-post; turn left along a grassy path between scrub, soon picking up and keeping by a wire fence on the left, to a stile. Climb it and continue along the left-hand edge of a field, by a wire fence and hedge on the left, bearing left to climb a stile at the bottom end.

Bear right to follow the direction of a yellow waymark across a field, heading towards East Bexington Farm and going through a metal gate in the bottom corner of the field. Follow the track ahead through another metal gate and continue, passing to the left of the farm buildings and curving right to cross a track. Keeping straight ahead, go through a metal gate and follow the track along the right-hand edge of a field, heading directly towards the sea.

On reaching the coast, turn left (**D**), signposted 'Coast Path and Abbotsbury', along a rough tarmac track. Follow this track (later a tarmac lane) for 1 mile (1.5 km), at first above Chesil Beach and later below the shingle embankment. Chesil Beach is a long, narrow embankment of pebbles and shingle, around 60 feet (18 m) above the sea at its highest point, stretching eastwards to the Isle of Portland. Beyond Abbotsbury it completely encloses a salt-water lagoon called the Fleet. The formation of this geological curiosity is something of a puzzle.

At the point where the tarmac lane turns to the left, keep ahead to pass beside a metal gate and on along a shingle path with a hedge on the left. Go through a gate and continue, between a hedge on the left and a wire fence on the right, along a track that runs along the edge of the Fleet Sanctuary Nature Reserve. Follow the track as it turns left to head inland and directly in front is a good view of St Catherine's Chapel. At a finger-post turn right (**E**) over a stile, signposted 'Coast Path and Swannery', and walk uphill across a field, heading towards and then keeping by a wire fence on the right, to a gate. Go through and follow the grassy path ahead, with a fine view to the

right of the swannery below and across the Fleet to Chesil Beach. Bear slightly left to climb a stile. Now continue along a delightful path below a wooded hill on the left, climbing a stile at the end of the trees.

Continue along the path to Abbotsbury and, just before reaching a metal kissing-gate (**F**), turn sharp left to follow the clearly defined uphill track to St Catherine's Chapel, a ½ mile (0.75 km) diversion worthwhile both for the chapel itself and for the views from its hilltop site. The chapel was built around 1400 by the monks of Abbotsbury Abbey and was probably used by visitors as a place of prayer before descending to the abbey itself. After the dissolution of the monasteries, the chapel was retained, probably because of its value as a landmark for sailors. It has an almost fortress-like appearance with great buttresses, and it is noted for its rare, stone, tunnel-vaulted roof. The all-round views are magnificent, especially looking towards Abbotsbury below, cradled amidst the downs and dominated by its church.

From the chapel, retrace your steps downhill to rejoin the main route and go through the metal kissing-gate (**F**). Continue along a broad track to a road, turn right and take the first turning on the right to return to your starting point. ☐

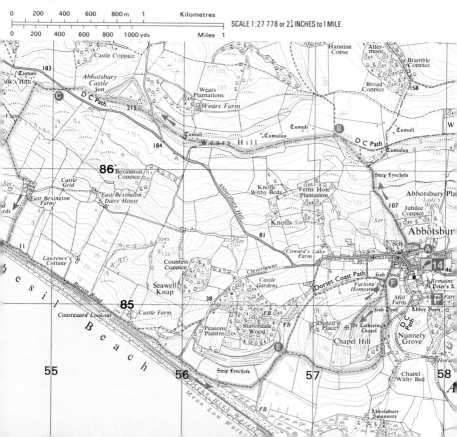

15 Badbury Rings and Kingston Lacy

Start:	National Trust car park at Badbury Rings, 3½ miles (5.5 km) north-west of Wimborne Minster
Distance:	7 miles (11.25 km)
Approximate time:	3½ hours
Parking:	Badbury Rings
Refreshments:	Café at Pamphill Farm Shop (just before Kingston Lacy church)
Ordnance Survey maps:	Landranger 195 (Bournemouth & Purbeck) and Pathfinder 1300, ST 80/90 (Blandford Forum)

General description *Wide and sweeping vistas are the chief characteristic of this walk that starts at the splendid prehistoric fort of Badbury Rings and takes you through attractive stretches of woodland, skirting the edge of Kingston Lacy Park. Much of the walk is on National Trust property, part of a large estate bequeathed to the Trust in 1981. The last part of the route crosses Badbury Rings and walkers are informed that dogs are not allowed here at any time because of sheep grazing.*

Badbury Rings is one of the most impressive Iron Age forts in the country. Its three great concentric ramparts are well preserved and encompass a huge area: the circumference of the fort is nearly 1 mile (1.5 km) and some of the ditches are over 60 feet (18 m) deep. Alongside the fort is Ackling Dyke, part of a Roman road that ran from Dorchester to Old Sarum.

Two stony tracks lead north-eastwards from the car park; take the one furthest away from the ramparts of Badbury Rings. Pass beside a wooden barrier and, about 100 yards (91 m) beyond that (where the stony track bears right), keep straight ahead along a grassy track, parallel to a wire fence on the left. At the end of the open grassy area, head downhill to pass beside a gate, by a bridleway sign, and continue along a fence-lined path, making for the woodland in front. All around, and indeed for most of the walk, there are fine and expansive views across sweeping downland.

The path continues through the woodland called the Oaks, crosses a track, and continues to a T-junction of tracks at the end of the woods. Here turn left to walk along a broad, straight, gently undulating and hedge-lined track that follows the line of the Roman Ackling Dyke across King Down. At a junction of tracks and paths (by a blue waymark), the Roman road continues ahead as a grassy track but you follow the broad track to the right (**A**) to continue across the down. Keep ahead at a meeting of three tracks, bear slightly right at a fork, and continue to where the track ends near buildings. Here go through the metal gate in front of you to continue along a hedge-lined tarmac lane, following it first around a left-hand bend, then a right-hand bend, and finally taking the right-hand lane at a fork down to the main road (**B**).

Cross the road and walk along the lane opposite (signposted 'Cowgrove, Pamphill and Kingston Lacy Church'), passing Pamphill Farm Shop and the early twentieth-century Kingston Lacy church. The lane keeps alongside the wooded boundary of Kingston Lacy Park for nearly 1 mile (1.5 km)

before turning sharply to the left. At this point (**C**) keep ahead and pass beside a gate to continue along a broad, straight track, still keeping by the left-hand edge of the park. Kingston Lacy House is invisible from the track as the park is surrounded by woodland, but it is well worth a visit at the end of the walk. It is a fine seventeenth-century mansion, built by Sir Ralph Bankes to replace the destroyed Corfe Castle, and has been recently restored by the National Trust.

At a T-junction of tracks, turn right and, where the track forks, continue along the right-hand track, still following the park boundary. This very attractive hedge- and tree-lined track eventually leads up to a metal gate and onto the main road (**D**). Turn right for a few yards and then, at the entrance to Lodge Farm, a superb example of a fourteenth-century hunting lodge, bear left along a track that passes to the right of the farm and continues to a yellow-waymarked stile. Climb this and keep along the left-hand edge of a field, by a hedge on the left, following the field edge around to the left. In front is High Wood and just to the left the tree-topped earthworks of Badbury Rings can be seen. Pass through a hedge gap, continue along the left-hand edge of the next

field and, at the end of the field, turn left to keep along the left-hand edge of High Wood. From here Kingston Lacy House can just be glimpsed across the fields on the left.

Continue to a T-junction (**E**), turn right for a few yards, and then turn left to climb a stile by a notice that says 'No dogs at any time'. Now head across rough meadowland to Badbury Rings and, after negotiating the steep ramparts, you can either follow the inner ramparts around or make your way across the middle of the fort to return to the car park. □

SCALE 1:27 778 or 2¼ INCHES to 1 MILE

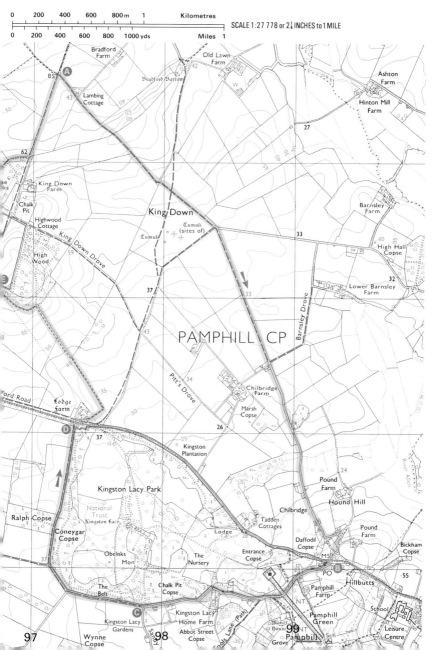

97   98   99

16 Cerne Abbas and Minterne Magna

Start:	Kettle Bridge picnic area on the edge of Cerne Abbas
Distance:	6½ miles (10.5 km)
Approximate time:	3½ hours
Parking:	Kettle Bridge picnic area
Refreshments:	Pubs and cafés at Cerne Abbas
Ordnance Survey maps:	Landranger 194 (Dorchester & Weymouth) and Pathfinder 1299, ST 60/70 (Cerne Abbas & Hazelbury Bryan)

General description *Historic interest and superb scenery are combined on this splendid downland walk. From Cerne Abbas a footpath heads up onto the downs, passing below the prehistoric figure of the Cerne Giant, and continues across open country and through woodland, with fine sweeping views, before descending into Minterne Magna. A short and easy climb onto a ridge is followed by a descent into the tiny hamlet of Up Cerne and a final stretch along a quiet lane back to Cerne Abbas. It is on this last leg that you see the classic view of the Cerne Giant on the opposite hillside.*

From the Kettle Bridge picnic area turn left along the lane for a few yards and just before a bridge turn right to follow a delightful tarmac path beside the tree-lined River Cerne into the village. Where the path forks, turn left over a footbridge and continue along the path ahead to emerge into Abbey Street (**A**). The church and village centre are to the right.

It is difficult to believe that the now quiet backwater of Cerne Abbas was once an important centre for the leather and brewing industries. It declined in the nineteenth century and what we have today is an exceptionally attractive village of stone and flint with some fine Georgian houses and, unusual for Dorset, a group of timber-fronted cottages in Abbey Street. The mainly fifteenth-century church is a graceful and spacious building with an imposing west tower. Of the once great Benedictine monastery, founded in 987, there are only fragmentary remains of the abbey itself, but a gatehouse and guest-house survive, plus an impressive fourteenth-century tithe barn on the other side of the village.

Turn left towards the abbey ruins and, just after passing to the left of a duck pond, turn right through a metal gate in an archway and follow a diagonal path across a cemetery to go through a similar metal gate in another archway. Keep in the same direction across a field, with the abbey remains on the left, and head uphill towards trees and the base of the hill on which the Cerne Giant is carved. Climb a stile and, ignoring another stile on the left, continue quite steeply uphill along a clearly defined path to a Cerne Giant National Trust sign.

Continue along a path by the wire fence enclosing the giant on the right. The possibility of damage by the feet of visitors means that it cannot be inspected closely and it is impossible to see anything as you pass below. All the way along there are grand views to the left over the wide and sweeping Cerne valley. Where the wire fence ends, keep ahead contouring along the side of Giant Hill, roughly parallel to a hedge below on the left. Bear slightly away from the hedge to follow a broad green ledge over the shoulder of the hill, continuing upwards between bushes into an open grassy area, to the left of which is a blue-waymarked post. Now keep along the right-hand edge of gorse bushes to climb a stile, turn half-left and head across a large open field (no visible path), making for a waymarked gatepost by the right-hand edge of a group of trees. Continue in the direction of the yellow (not the blue) waymarking arrows along the left-hand edge of a field, by a hedge on the left, now following an obvious path to a stile, and climb it onto a road (**B**).

Turn left along the road for ¼ mile (0.5 km) and at the end of a group of fine old trees on the left, turn left through a gate, then turn half-right and head across to a fence corner. Go through a gate and continue along the left-hand edge of a field high above the valley, by a wire fence on the left, later keeping above a narrow belt of woodland on the left to reach a T-junction (**C**). Here turn left to walk along a fine, broad, ridge-top track, with splendid views both sides over rolling country; to the left Minterne House is prominent in the valley below. Follow the track through a circular wooded area, which contains the earthworks of Dogbury Camp, after which the track heads downhill to a road.

Turn left onto the road and, in front of a house, turn left again through a wooden gate (**D**). Go through a waymarked metal gate a few yards in front and head straight across a large sloping field (no path), keeping roughly parallel to and about 100 yards (91 m) above a fence on the right. Go through the next metal gate and keep in the same direction across the next field, parallel to a wire fence on the right, along a narrow but discernible

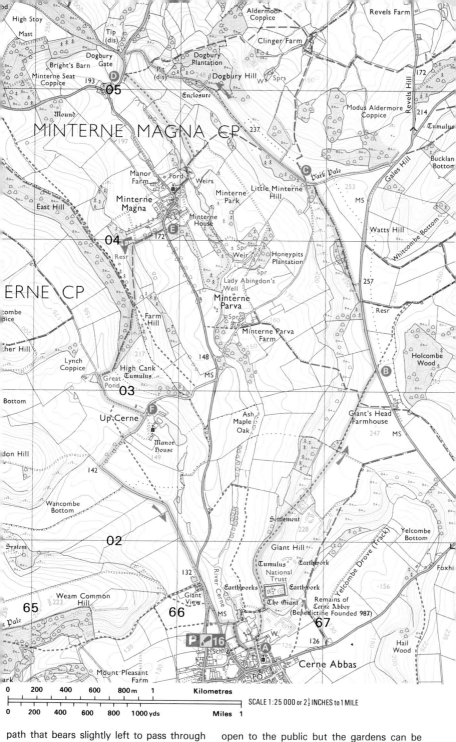

path that bears slightly left to pass through another metal gate. Afterwards the path bears right and continues across the next field to a metal gate; go through it and turn right along a downhill track. Ahead is Minterne House, a large mansion built around the beginning of the century. It is not open to the public but the gardens can be visited during the summer months. The track bears left to cross a footbridge over a stream and continues into the village of Minterne Magna, passing by the small fifteenth-century church.

Turn left along the main road that curves to

Cerne Giant, a distinctive prehistoric figure cut from
the chalk hillside

17 Bryants Puddle Heath and Moreton

Start:	Forestry Commission car park at Cull-peppers Dish ½ mile (0.75 km) south of Briantspuddle
Distance:	7 miles (11.25 km)
Approximate time:	3½ hours
Parking:	Cull-peppers Dish
Refreshments:	None
Ordnance Survey maps:	Landranger 194 (Dorchester & Weymouth) and Outdoor Leisure 15 (Purbeck)

General description *The initial impression that most of this route will be through uninteresting conifer plantations is soon dispelled; the conifers themselves are interspersed with patches of open heathland, and the latter part of the walk includes some lovely meadowland near Moreton and fine deciduous woodland. This is very much 'Lawrence of Arabia' country: the walk passes both his house and his grave.*

Cull-peppers Dish, from which the parking area takes its unusual name, is the large, tree-filled hollow on the other side of the road, formed naturally through subsidence and one of several similar features in the area. From the car park turn left along the road and, at the blue-waymarked post, turn right to follow a path into the trees. On meeting a track turn half-right and walk along it in a straight line, taking care to keep on the main track all the while. Head downhill, bear left on joining another track in front of a house, soon bearing right and continuing down to a road (**A**).

Turn left if you want to visit the pleasant, sleepy, thatched village of Briantspuddle; otherwise turn right uphill along the road. At a junction keep left to reach a crossroads and continue ahead along a straight road between conifers, signposted to Bovington, for ½ mile (0.75 km) to reach a T-junction (**B**). Here take the narrow but clear sandy path ahead across an area of heathland dotted with conifers, part of Thomas Hardy's Egdon Heath.

On joining a wider track, keep ahead (there are lots of Ministry of Defence 'Out of Bounds' notices around here, as this is part of a tank-training area), looking out for a blue waymark on a tree, which directs you to bear right off this broad track onto another one.

the right through the village and, just after the road bends to the left, turn right through a metal gate (**E**) and walk along a straight, tree-lined track, heading up to another metal gate. Go through that, turn left for a few yards by a fence on the left, and then bear right to head diagonally uphill across a sloping field, making for a metal gate in the far corner. Go through and keep in the same direction across the corner of the next field to go through a waymarked gate onto a track a few yards ahead. Turn left and almost immediately bear right at a fork along a grassy tree-lined track that heads downhill, curving right to a T-junction in front of the Great Pond.

Turn left along a tarmac track into the secluded thatched hamlet of Up Cerne (**F**). Here there is the traditional and highly picturesque scene of manor house and church side by side, beautifully situated above a lake. The church dates from the fifteenth century and the manor house mainly from the sixteenth century, but both were heavily restored in the nineteenth century.

Turn right along a quiet and narrow lane, at first uphill, then gently downhill and finally around a sharp left-hand bend to continue along to the main road. Bear right and about 100 yards (91 m) ahead is the junction and lay-by at Giant View. From here is the best view of the Cerne Giant, a prehistoric male nude figure, 180 feet (55 m) tall, cut out of the chalk hillside. The erect phallus indicates that the figure was associated with fertility and not surprisingly many stories have grown up around it, notably that making love on the figure or simply sitting on the tip of the phallus was a cure for barrenness.

From Giant View take the left fork, signposted 'Village Centre', and take the first turning on the left to return to the starting point.   □

Affpuddle
West Farm
East Farm
War
Meml
Sch
Shop
Farm
Briantspuddle
Briantspuddle
Farm
Throop
River Piddle or Trent
Ford
FB
FB
FB
Brockhil

93

P X

AFFPUDDLE CP
Cull-peppers
Dish
285
238
17
Throop Clump
Tumulus

Affpuddle
Heath
P X
Tumuli
290
W
Throop Heath
TUR
PUDD
Tumulus

92
Rimsmoor
Pond
182
Bryants Puddle Heath
152
Tumulus

Oakers Wood
Oakers Wood
House
Moreton Plantation
Tonerspuddle Heath
Tumulus

Bound Stone
Plantation
Oakers Wood
Cottage
F
P
P
190
C
230
NT
Lawrence of Arabia's
Cottage
289
Tumulus

91
Spr
Spyway
Clouds Hill
231

Two Gates
FB
Ford
D
Te

90
194
187

River Frome
Oak
The Glade
E
Bovington Heath
200

Mill
Ford
P
81
Snelling
Farm
82
Foxbury
83

reton
sch
Manor
House
Cemy
93
Moreton
House
FBs
Tumuli
Cranes Moor

LAWRENCE
F ARABIA'S
GRAVE
89

0   200   400   600   800m   1
Kilometres

0   200   400   600   800   1000 yds
Miles   1

SCALE 1:25 000 or 2½ INCHES to 1 MILE

The next turning is difficult to spot. After about 100 yards (91 m) (roughly half-way between the first and second 'Out of Bounds' notices on the right), bear right onto a narrow and rather indistinct path, overgrown in places with heather and bracken. Head gently uphill across rough heathland, making for two prominent dead trees that act as useful landmarks; all around are extensive views over forest and heath. Pass to the left of the trees and continue in a straight line, finally heading through an area overgrown with rhododendrons to emerge onto a road at a T-junction (C).

Keep ahead, signposted 'Clouds Hill and Tank Museum', passing to the right of Clouds Hill, the former home of Lawrence of Arabia. T.E. Lawrence first bought this small, plain and isolated cottage in 1925 when stationed at nearby Bovington Camp, but he only came to live here permanently in 1935, just two months before his fatal motor-cycle accident. It is now a National Trust property.

After nearly ½ mile (0.75 km) you reach a small car park on the left on the edge of a tank-training area. Here turn right (D) at a yellow waymark and 'Warning' and 'Royal Tank Corps' notices, and walk along a sandy track, by a wire fence on the right. After a while you bear right and keep a look-out for a yellow-waymarked post and notice for the Royal Tank Corps Centre, where you turn right onto a very pleasant woodland path. Head downhill to join a wide sandy track, bear left along it, pass beside a metal barrier to a T-junction of tracks, and turn right to follow a track through an area of mixed woodland. Turn right again at the next T-junction, with attractive views now across wide, flat meadows and sheep pastures, and at the next T-junction follow a yellow waymark to the left.

Look out for a waymarked stile on the right (E). The main route continues over this stile, but it is worth while making a short detour into the village of Moreton. In order to do this keep ahead, bearing left to cross an arm of the River Frome, taking the right-hand track at a fork and later crossing a footbridge over the main river to continue into the village. To the left is the interesting church, built in the Georgian Gothic style in 1776, enlarged in the nineteenth century and restored after extensive bomb damage in the Second World War. A little further on to the right is the cemetery that contains the grave of Lawrence of Arabia.

Retrace your steps to the waymarked stile (E) and turn left over it to rejoin the main route. Immediately turn half-right and head diagonally across a field, clipping a fence corner and bearing right to a stile. Climb it, keep ahead across the next field. Then climb another stile and continue straight ahead,

The River Frome near Moreton

climbing two more stiles in quick succession and the intervening plank over a ditch. After heading across the next field, you climb a stile on the edge of woodland, cross a plank over another ditch, and climb another stile. Now follow a well waymarked path that winds through the trees to reach a track just to the right of some ruined buildings. Turn left and the track soon bears right to continue along the left-hand edge of woodland, passing through a metal gate onto a road (F).

Cross the road and take the broad track opposite at a bridleway sign to Cull-peppers Dish. The track passes through the lovely broadleaved Oakers Wood. Where the track bends right to Oakers Wood House, keep straight ahead (there is a blue waymark on a tree) along a narrower woodland path. Keep following blue waymarks all the time, later entering the conifers of Bryants Puddle Heath and heading uphill.

Where a blue-waymarked post indicates a path junction, keep ahead – Rimsmoor Pond can be seen below on the right – and after about 50 yards (46 m), bear left onto a narrow and indistinct path through bracken. It is not easy to spot this junction, but a short distance ahead is a prominent blue-waymarked post where you cross a track. After crossing this track keep ahead, climbing quite steeply to reach another track just before emerging onto a road. Turn right back to the start. □

18 Eype Down and Thorncombe Beacon

followed by an exhilarating climb over Thorncombe Beacon, along one of the most spectacular stretches of the Dorset coast, to conclude a highly scenic and quite energetic walk.

Start:	Eype Mouth
Distance:	6 miles (9.5 km)
Approximate time:	3 hours
Parking:	Eype Mouth
Refreshments:	Cafés at Eype Mouth, pubs and cafés at Chideock, pub at Seatown
Ordnance Survey maps:	Landranger 193 (Taunton & Lyme Regis) and Pathfinder 1317, SY 49/59 (Bridport)

General description From Eype Mouth you head inland, first over Eype Down and then over Quarry Hill, before descending into Chideock. Then comes the one flat part of the walk to rejoin the coast at Seatown,

Start by walking up the lane away from the beach and, where the lane bends to the right, turn left through a gate, at a Down House Farm National Trust sign and Eype Down footpath sign (**A**). Walk along a track to the left of bungalows, climb a stile, and continue along the grassy track ahead, by a hedge on the right, bearing right to go through a gate at a footpath sign. Continue steadily uphill, go through a gate, and keep ahead to pass through another gate onto a track.

Turn left along the track to a farm and, at a footpath sign, turn sharp right onto a track in the direction of Eype Down. Follow this broad, wooded track uphill, curving gradually to the right and, a few yards before reaching a metal gate, bear left to follow a grassy path through the gorse, bracken, grassland and scattered trees of Eype Down. From these bracing heights the views are superb. At a path junction by a footpath sign, keep ahead

along a narrow winding path, signposted to Quarry Hill and Chideock, which continues across the down, later heading downhill to a track. Bear right to cross with care the busy A35 a few yards ahead (**B**) and continue along the narrow lane opposite, signposted 'Quarr Lane No Through Road'.

Where the lane bears right, keep straight ahead along a hedge-lined track, go through a metal gate, and turn left to follow a grassy track up Quarry Hill, by a line of trees on the left. To the left are fine views over the coast, with Seatown nestling in the hollow between the twin cliffs of Golden Cap to the right and Thorncombe Beacon to the left. Bear right to follow the track across the open hilltop (there are regular footpath signs). The uneven ground and hollows are evidence of the former quarrying activities, though now mostly grassed over, and the hill is attractive in itself as well as providing outstanding views both inland and over the coast. Continue along the grassy track as it winds over the hilltop, but watch out for a footpath sign that directs you to the left to start heading downhill towards Chideock, through a gully between two flanks of the hill.

Turn right over a stile that can be seen just below, and head downhill across a field, making for a stile in the bottom corner. Climb it, and keep ahead a few yards to another stile, path junction and footpath sign. Here turn left to follow a downhill track, go through a metal gate, and continue along a track that curves to the right past a farm building and then bears left, now becoming a concrete drive. Soon the drive turns left and heads down to rejoin the A35 on the edge of Chideock (**C**).

Turn right and keep ahead for the amenities of Chideock: thatched cottages, pubs, cafés and a fifteenth-century church. After about 50 yards (46 m), the main route turns left at a footpath sign to Seatown, following a hedge-lined path to a stile. Climb it and keep along the right-hand edge of a field, by a hedge on the right, to cross first a footbridge and then a stile. Bear slightly left across the next field (it sometimes has caravans) to climb another stile. Turn half-right, in the direction of a footpath sign to Seatown, cross a track, and walk along a straight, grassy path between fences. Bear left through a metal kissing-gate to continue along the left-hand edge of a sewage plant. Keep ahead along a concrete drive for a few yards, cross a stream and, at a footpath sign 'Seatown and Beach', turn left through a kissing-gate. Head across a field, cross a track and keep ahead to go through another kissing-gate. Cross a footbridge, continue ahead to join a concrete track, and follow this to a lane.

Turn left down to the beach at Seatown and, at a 'Coast Path' sign to Eype, turn left (**D**) down some steps, cross a footbridge, and head across a car park to climb a stile at a National Trust sign for Ridge Cliff. Now you follow the coast path back to Eype Mouth, climbing several stiles and enjoying outstanding views all the way. At first you climb steeply onto Ridge Cliff, continue over Doghouse Hill and then on up to Thorncombe Beacon. Here is one of the most spectacular of views: almost the whole length of the Dorset coast is stretched out before you, from Chesil Beach in the east to Golden Cap and across Lyme Bay to the Devon coast in the west. In addition the views inland are equally grand.

From here head downhill along the cliff edge to return to Eype Mouth. ☐

Thorncombe Beacon

19 Eggardon Hill and Powerstock Common

Start:	Shatcombe Lane picnic area on Eggardon Hill, 200 yards (183 m) east of junction with lane between Toller Porcorum and A35
Distance:	8½ miles (13.5 km)
Approximate time:	4½ hours
Parking:	Shatcombe Lane picnic area
Refreshments:	Spyway Inn at point E, pub at Nettlecombe, pub at Powerstock
Ordnance Survey maps:	Landranger 194 (Dorchester & Weymouth) and Pathfinder 1317, SY 49/59 (Bridport)

General description *The bare and austere slopes of Eggardon Hill, crowned by the extensive ramparts of an Iron Age fort, command magnificent views over both downland and coast. Starting at the top of the hill, the route descends below the earthworks of the fort into a valley and continues along field paths, tracks and lanes to the picturesque village of Powerstock. From there a gentle climb through the woodlands of Powerstock Common, a relic of a medieval forest, enables you to regain the ridge and return to Eggardon Hill.*

Refer to map overleaf.

From the car park and picnic area walk for a short distance along the lane to a T-junction and turn left. Immediately there is a superb view to the right over downland, with the woods of Powerstock Common in the valley below. Turn right at the next junction, signposted to Powerstock and West Milton, and look out for a waymarked gate on the left (**A**). Go through this and follow the direction of the blue arrow across grass to the fort, going through a metal gate and turning right for a few yards along a track. The fort is one of the most impressive and spectacularly sited of all the Iron Age forts in Dorset — many people consider it more atmospheric than the better-known Maiden Castle.

In front of another metal gate bear left and ahead you will see two stiles. Climb the right-hand one to explore the fort; to continue the walk, climb the left-hand one and walk downhill along a splendid, broad, grassy track, with superb views over the valley to the left looking towards the coast, keeping by a wire fence on the left and below the earthworks of the fort on the right. Having passed a high, outlying embankment on the left, turn sharp left and go through a metal gate. Follow the path downhill, at first between hedges and then, after passing through a gate into an open field, keep alongside a hedge and embankment on the right. Go through another gate, keep ahead a few yards, and then turn left in front of farm buildings onto a rough track (**B**).

Follow the track, keeping the farm buildings on the right. The track bends first right and then left following the building line. Go through a gate and bear left along a partially concreted track. This track turns left to a private house, but you should keep ahead along a broad, grassy path. Go through the gate at the end of the path and then bear slightly right across a field to another gate. The surface beyond is boggy, with a bank and hedge on the left and a drainage ditch on the right. Keep ahead, going through another gate and then into a field with views of South Eggardon Farm in the valley bottom. Head downhill across the field and go through a gate, after which the path drops steeply and then bears right to run a few yards along the side of a small stream (the ground here is very wet underfoot). Enter a field through a small blue-waymarked gate; the stream here flows into a pond on the left. Walk round the pond and then across a sleeper bridge that spans the exit stream from the pond. Climb up the hill and, after going through two gates, turn right onto a farm track (**C**). Keep to this track, which ends in a gate that admits you to a road (**D**). Turn right downhill past the Spyway Inn.

About 50 yards (46 m) beyond the inn take a track on the right signposted to Powerstock (**E**). Keep ahead a few yards and then go through a metal gate into a field where there is an electricity pylon. Keep to the left-hand fence and beyond the pylon you will see fine views of the Eggardon Hill fort on the skyline ahead. At the corner of the field, go through a gate and follow the track ahead, going first downhill, then across a stream, and finally up into another field. Keep to the track along the left-hand edge of the field, go through another gate, and bear left to the edge of the next field. Then follow the left-hand fence, beyond which is a wooded ravine complete with stream; listen and look for woodpeckers. Keep alongside the fence until a gate is reached that leads out onto a track (**F**). Turn left and follow that track for nearly 1 mile (1.5 km). Later, the track becomes a tarmac lane that descends gently to pass under a disused railway bridge and then heads uphill equally gently. A few yards after the lane flattens out, turn right (**G**) through a gate, turn left over a stile, and walk diagonally across a field to go through a gate in the far corner. Immediately climb the stone stile in front onto a lane and turn right into the thatched hamlet of Nettlecombe.

Bear left at the first junction and at the next junction turn right through a gate beside the Marquis of Lorne pub and at a public footpath sign to Powerstock (**H**). Ahead is a glorious view of Powerstock village. Keep along the right-hand edge of a field, by a wire fence on the right, and where the fence bears right, continue straight ahead, descending steeply into a valley. Go through a gate, cross a footbridge over a stream, and bear slightly right across a meadow to go through another gate. Cross a further footbridge over another stream and keep ahead along an uphill path, between a wall on the left and a hedge on the right, to a lane (**J**).

The village is just to the left. In a county noted for its large number of attractive villages, Powerstock ranks as one of the most picturesque, with stone and thatched cottages grouped at random on different levels. Overlooking the village is the church, mostly rebuilt in 1859 but still retaining a richly ornamented Norman chancel arch from the original twelfth-century structure.

The route continues to the right along the narrow lane, passing below the grassy slopes of a Norman motte and bailey castle. Follow the lane for nearly 1 mile (1.5 km) and, where it bears to the right by a bridleway sign to Stones Common, keep ahead to a gate (**K**). Go through, pass in front of a farmhouse, go through a metal gate, and keep straight ahead across grass. Go through another gate to enter woodland and follow a path at first through a conifer plantation, later continuing uphill through delightful broadleaved woodland mostly of oak and ash. This is a remnant of the medieval Powerstock Forest, created a royal forest by King John and now a Dorset Naturalists' Trust Reserve. The

The Iron Age fort on Eggardon Hill broods over the surrounding countryside

path, narrow but reasonably well defined, winds upwards to emerge into an area of open grassland and bracken on the right-hand edge of the trees before continuing gently uphill. Where it flattens out, look out for a blue-waymarked gate a few yards to the right (**L**).

Go through the gate and walk in a straight line across the middle of a large field, heading downhill, and on the far side turn right alongside a wire fence down to a metal gate

SCALE 1:25 000 or 2½ INCHES to 1 MILE

in the bottom corner. Go through and continue along a broad uphill track to Barrowland Farm, here going through two metal gates in quick succession. Turn right along a track, passing to the right of the farmhouse, and at the end of the farm buildings continue straight ahead. Go through a metal gate and keep in the same direction, heading diagonally uphill across a field (no visible path) to go through a gate in the far corner. Bear right along the right-hand

edge of a field, by a wire fence and above a steep wooded bank on the right, and where the field edge curves to the right, continue in the same direction across the field, making for a metal gate about half-way along its far edge.

Go through the gate, turn left and go through another one a few yards ahead onto a lane (**M**). Turn right along the lane for ½ mile (0.75 km) and turn left at the first junction to return to the parking area. □

20 Golden Cap

Start:	Seatown
Distance:	6½ miles (10.5 km)
Approximate time:	3½ hours
Parking:	Seatown
Refreshments:	Pub at Seatown
Ordnance Survey maps:	Landranger 193 (Taunton & Lyme Regis), Pathfinders 1316, SY 29/39 (Lyme Regis & Axminster) and 1317, SY 49/59 (Bridport)

General description Most of the coast between Seatown and Charmouth is owned by the National Trust, and a combination of clear, well maintained paths and good waymarking, plus outstanding cliff scenery and spectacular views along the coast and inland, make this excellent walking country. Golden Cap is, at 626 ft (191 m), the highest point on the south coast of England and is inevitably a superb viewpoint. Its name comes from the layer of golden sandstone that crowns its distinctive flat summit. This is quite an energetic walk, with several ascents and descents, but the only stiff climb is the final one, up to the top of Golden Cap itself, the highlight of the walk.

Start by the beach at Seatown. Facing the sea, turn right at a 'Coast Path' sign for Golden Cap and Charmouth, and walk along the edge of the low cliffs. Ahead is the first of a series of superb views of Golden Cap seen from many different angles. Climb up steps to a National Trust sign to 'West Cliff' and continue along the cliff, heading uphill to a finger-post (**A**). Here bear right off the coast path, following directions to Langdon Hill and Chideock, climb a stile about 50 yards (46 m) ahead, and continue uphill by a wire fence on the right to reach a stile in front of the dark woodlands of Langdon Hill.

Climb the stile, turn left along a path that keeps by the left-hand edge of the wood, and go through a gate at the end of the trees. Follow the left-hand hedge past the path to Golden Cap, keep around the bank to a post facing the sea, and continue along a grassy path by a hedge on the left. To the right is rolling downland and ahead a fine view looking across Lyme Bay to Lyme Regis. About 50 yards (46 m) before reaching the end of the field, bear right across the field corner to a stile. Do not climb it, but turn right, following the directions of a finger-post to St Gabriel's, along the field edge by a wire fence

on the left, heading downhill. In the bottom corner of the field, turn left through a gate to follow a track along the right-hand bottom edge of a sloping field, with a hedge on the right, passing below the summit of Golden Cap to reach the scanty remains of St Gabriel's Church, a small thirteenth-century building that became ruined when its congregation gradually moved away to less isolated settlements nearby.

Bear right past the ruins to climb a stile and continue for a short distance along a track as far as a finger-post by a fine thatched farmhouse (**B**). Turn right, in the direction of Morcombelake and Stonebarrow, along a concrete track that crosses a stream and heads uphill, lined by hedges on both sides, later curving right and levelling off. Go through a gate, keep ahead along what is now a rough, stony track and, at a crossroads, turn left signposted Stonebarrow and Charmouth. Head gently up towards Upcot Farm, turn right to pass to the right of the farmhouse, and continue along an uphill track, by the left-hand edge of woodland, to a finger-post.

Keep ahead, passing through two gates and following the track around a left-hand curve at a bridleway sign. Continue uphill towards the ridge, climb a stile, and bear right along a faint, grassy track across open, gorse-strewn grassland. Go through a gate

56

by a finger-post, keep ahead a few yards to another finger-post, and bear left (**C**) along a broad track signposted to Stonebarrow and Charmouth. Now follow this splendid ridge-top track for just over ½ mile (0.75 km) across an area of grass, gorse, bracken and low trees, with grand views to the left over the sea and later to the right across Marshwood Vale and the hills of west Dorset, to reach the National Trust parking area at Stonebarrow Hill.

Continue through the car park, passing the National Trust shop and information point, and at the far end bear left across grass to a line of trees to turn left (**D**) through a gap in a fence. With a fine view of Golden Cap to the left, walk along a broad, grassy path, between a tree-topped bank on the right and gorse bushes on the left, heading downhill towards farm buildings. The path bears left and continues downhill to join a concrete track. Here you turn right, signposted 'Westhay and Coast Path', along to Westhay Farm. Passing to the left of the farm buildings, keep straight ahead along a grassy path, go through a gate, and continue across open grassland, making for a finger-post.

Here turn left (**E**) to join the coast path to Seatown; the path is easy to follow as the route keeps along the top of the undulating cliffs and is well waymarked, with regular finger-posts and stiles. Head directly for

Golden Cap, the highest point on the south coast of England

Golden Cap, climbing quite steeply up to the summit plateau and heading across it, passing the memorial stone to the Earl of Antrim, Chairman of the National Trust 1966–77, to reach the triangulation pillar (**F**). The views from here, inland and along the coast in both directions, are magnificent, extending from Chesil Beach in the east and across Lyme Bay to Lyme Regis and the Devon coast in the west.

From here descend abruptly via a series of steps, climb a stile, and turn right at a 'Coast Path and Seatown' sign. Continue downhill, following 'Coast Path' signs for the final mile (1.5 km) back to Seatown, joining the outward route towards the end. ☐

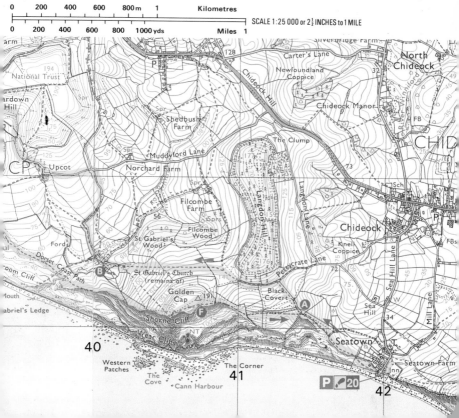

21 Ashmore and Stubhampton Bottom

Start:	Ashmore
Distance:	8 miles (12.75 km)
Approximate time:	4 hours
Parking:	By the pond at Ashmore
Refreshments:	None
Ordnance Survey maps:	Landrangers 184 (Salisbury & The Plain) and 195 (Bournemouth & Purbeck), Pathfinder 1281, ST 81/91 (Shillingstone & Tollard Royal)

General description *Much of this walk is through splendid woodland, a reminder of the former hunting ground of Cranborne Chase. From the hilltop village of Ashmore, you descend into the thickly wooded valley of Stubhampton Bottom. A fine walk through the valley is followed by a gentle ascent via Ashmore Bottom, continuing through more woodland to return to the start.*

Thatched cottages grouped around the village duck pond make an idyllic starting point to the walk at Ashmore, 718 feet (219 m) up on Cranborne Chase and the highest village in Dorset. Begin by walking along the lane, passing the war memorial and Victorian church. Just before reaching a 'Single Track' sign where the road bears to the right and starts to drop downhill, turn left (**A**) through a metal gate and into a field. Keep by the left-hand edge initially, but then bear right across the slope, aiming for a metal gate just to the left of a small conifer plantation.

Go through the gate and just after the plantation ends to your right, turn left (**B**) and cross a small stile over the wire fence into the adjoining field. Then turn right and follow the hedge line for approximately 250 yards (228 m) before turning right (**C**) and crossing another stile into a field which slopes away to the valley below. Turn left and continue along the left-hand edge of the field, making towards the trees in front and passing through a metal gate in the far corner. Keep ahead for a few yards to join a distinct track and bear left along it through the woodland. Follow this main track round to the left along an avenue of tall conifers backed by mixed woodland. Soon after emerging into a small clearing where another track joins from the left, turn right (**D**) off the main track and along a grassy path that curves through mixed woodland and then drops steeply downhill into Stubhampton Bottom (**E**).

Turn left along a track and follow it through the wooded valley bottom for the next 2 miles (3.25 km), keeping along the main track all the while. On reaching a field on the left, ignore a blue waymark directing you to the left, and continue ahead, emerging from woodland into more open country and eventually joining a lane. Keep along the lane for about 100 yards (91 m) and, at a bridleway sign to Ashmore, turn left (**F**) along a track through Ashmore Bottom, passing through a succession of metal gates. The sides of the valley are more gentle and open than at Stubhampton Bottom.

After going through a metal gate to enter woodland, immediately turn right (**G**) by a blue waymark on a tree, following an uphill path near the right-hand edge of the wood to reach a track. Turn left along this hedge-lined track as far as a broad, tarmac track and here turn right (**H**) at a yellow waymark to follow a grassy track between hedges and trees on the right and a wire fence on the left. The

An idyllic scene at Ashmore

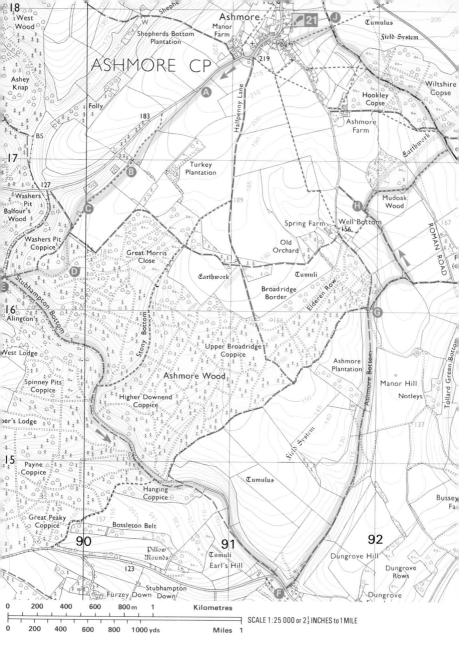

track bears right to keep along the right-hand edge of Mudoak Wood, following the edge of the wood around to the left and bearing right to a gate. Go through this and turn left along a downhill track, by a line of trees and wire fence on the left.

At the bottom corner of the field, turn left and negotiate a small, overgrown area to climb a makeshift stile in a wire fence and walk along the right-hand edge of a field, by a wire fence and trees on the right. Turn right over a stile, after a few yards turn left along a clear and distinct path and at a fork take the right-hand grassy path through the lovely woodlands of Wiltshire Copse, so named because it straddles the county boundary between Dorset and Wiltshire. Later keep along the edge of the woodland, by a wire fence on the left, to reach a stile. Climb this, keep ahead to climb another, and continue along an overgrown and indistinct path through a narrow belt of woodland.

When you see a stile on the left (**J**), climb it, and the village of Ashmore can be seen straight ahead. Follow a path between fences, go through a gate to the right of a house, and continue along a track to a lane. Turn right to return to the village pond. ☐

22 Worth Matravers, St Aldhelm's Head and Chapman's Pool

Start:	Worth Matravers
Distance:	7 ½ miles (12 km)
Approximate time:	4 hours
Parking:	Worth Matravers
Refreshments:	Pub and café at Worth Matravers
Ordnance Survey maps:	Landranger 195 (Bournemouth & Purbeck) and Outdoor Leisure 15 (Purbeck)

General description After crossing fields to reach the sea at Dancing Ledge, the route continues along one of the most spectacular stretches of the Purbeck coast, rounding the prominent headland at St Aldhelm's Chapel and passing above the beautiful Chapman's Pool. Both on the inland and coastal sections there is plenty of evidence of former extensive quarrying in this area. This is a fairly energetic walk with several steep ascents and descents, the most strenuous being just after St Aldhelm's Head.

The former quarrying village of Worth Matravers is a delightful place. Its grey stone cottages cluster around the village green and pond, and the church is one of the finest Norman churches in Dorset, particularly noted for its superb twelfth-century chancel arch.

From the car park above the village, turn right down the road and, on reaching a junction on the edge of the village, turn sharp left, following directions to Swanage and Langton Matravers. After ¼ mile (0.5 km), turn right over a stile (**A**) at a footpath sign to Eastington and Priest's Way, and head diagonally across the corner of a field to a stile. Climb this, cross a drive, climb another stile, and continue in the same direction

across the next field to climb a third stile. Keep along the right-hand edge of the next field, by a wire fence on the right, and where that fence meets a wall, bear slightly left and head across to a stone stile beside a gate and footpath sign.

Climb the stile to join the Priest's Way, a medieval route allegedly used by priests travelling between the church at Worth Matravers and Swanage. Follow a track, initially passing to the left of Eastington Farm, for almost 1 mile (1.5 km), a most attractive route with fine views to the left looking towards Langton Matravers with the Purbeck ridge on the horizon. The track, partially walled, passes some old quarry workings and there are several stiles to negotiate.

Just after passing a small pond on the right, turn right (**B**) over a stile at a footpath marker-stone to Dancing Ledge, and walk along a track, later keeping by a wall on the left. Where the wall ends, bear slightly left through a gap between the wall and a fence (do not take the path slightly to the right) and continue in the same direction, heading

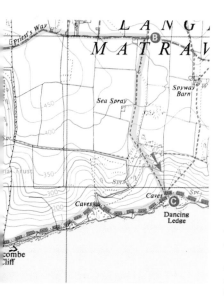

downhill between gorse bushes to a stile. Climb this and continue downhill to a stile in the bottom corner of the field, here joining the Dorset Coast Path (**C**). To the left, over a stile, is Dancing Ledge, a wide platform from which locally quarried stone used to be lowered onto boats. There are a number of similar 'ledges' or platforms all along this stretch of coast.

At a footpath marker-stone to Seacombe, turn right in front of a stile to follow a most

The beautiful cove of Chapman's Pool lies below Houns-tout Cliff

spectacular section of the coast path, noted for its outstanding limestone cliff scenery, for the next 4 miles (6.5 km). At first the path heads over Seacombe Cliff to descend into Seacombe Bottom. Here follow signs slightly inland along a track (this is to avoid Seacombe Quarry), before turning left up steps to regain the cliff top. Later the path descends into Winspit, where there are more quarry remains and ledges from which stone would be lowered onto boats to be transported to Swanage and then on to London. Another ascent is followed by a particularly lovely stretch to St Aldhelm's Head (**D**). The headland is 353 ft (108 m) high, with fine views, a coastguard station, cottages and an interesting little Norman chapel that has an unusually fine vaulted roof.

Here the coast path bears right around the headland (ignore the path to Worth and Renscombe that goes past the chapel) and now comes the steepest descent, followed by the steepest ascent of the walk. A series of steps aids progress while the spectacular cliff scenery ahead and a superb view over Chapman's Pool more than make up for the effort required. Soon after passing a memorial to the Royal Marines killed in action between 1945 and 1990, you reach a footpath marker-stone above Chapman's Pool, a beautiful little cove. For the energetic, or those with plenty of time, paths lead steeply down to the beach.

Turn right over a stile (**E**), in the direction of Renscombe, and walk across the field ahead to climb another stile and continue across the next field, bearing left near the far end to a further stile. Climb this, cross a track to climb the stile opposite, and walk along the left-hand edge of a field, by a wire fence on the left, to climb another stile. Continue along a narrow path towards a farm, climb a stile onto the farm drive and turn left along it to reach a lane.

Turn right into Worth Matravers, passing the church and pond, and bear left along the lane signposted to Kingston, Corfe Castle and Wareham to return to the car park. □

23 Bulbarrow Hill and Milton Abbas

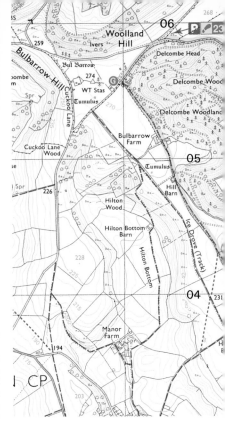

Start:	Car park and viewpoint on northern slopes of Bulbarrow Hill
Distance:	8 miles (12.75 km)
Approximate time:	4 hours
Parking:	Bulbarrow Hill
Refreshments:	Pub and café at Milton Abbas
Ordnance Survey maps:	Landranger 194 (Dorchester & Weymouth), Pathfinders 1299, ST 60/70 (Cerne Abbas & Hazelbury Bryan) and 1300, ST 80/90 (Blandford Forum)

General description *From the superb viewpoint of Bulbarrow Hill, you follow an undulating but mostly downhill route along tracks and short stretches of lane through quiet, wooded valleys, into the planned eighteenth-century estate village of Milton Abbas. From here you continue through landscaped parkland, passing Milton Abbey and the great house, before ascending across downland and through woodland to regain the top of Bulbarrow Hill. The open sweeping views and lovely stretches of woodland that punctuate the route complement the historic and architectural appeal of village and abbey to create an exceptionally interesting walk.*

Bulbarrow Hill is, at 899 feet (274 m), the second-highest point in Dorset and a magnificent viewpoint. From the car park the view stretches northwards across the patchwork landscape of Blackmoor Vale to the distant Black Down and Quantock Hills. An AA toposcope helps you to identify all the places that can be seen.

From the car park take the road signposted to Milton Abbas and Blandford Forum, following the boundary wall of Delcombe Wood on the right. Where the road forks, bear left (signposted Winterborne Stickland and Turnworth), and after 200 yards (183 m) turn right at a bridleway sign to go through a metal gate (**A**). Immediately turn half-left and head downhill across a field (there is no visible path), making for a dip where a gate marked with a bridleway sign admits you to Ochill Wood. Continue along a clear track through the wood, the first of a number of lovely stretches of woodland on this walk, heading gently downhill through the steep-sided, secluded valley. Go through a gate to leave the wood and continue along a pleasant grassy track, passing farmhouses and cottages. After the second farm, the grassy track becomes a tarmac one.

Continue to a crossroads of tracks; here the tarmac track turns left, but you turn right (**B**), by a half-hidden bridleway sign to Milton Abbas, along a track that later becomes tree-lined with hedge-banks on both sides, heading uphill over Houghton South Down. Go through a metal gate to a bridleway sign and from here keep ahead across an open grassy area, with fine views to the right of rolling, well-wooded downs. Curve gradually to the left to reach a metal gate in the top left-hand corner of the grassland by trees. Go through the gate, walk along a track, and go through another metal gate onto a road. Turn right and, just before reaching a junction, turn left (**C**) through a metal gate and head downhill along the right-hand side of a field, by a wire fence on the right.

Go through a metal gate to enter the mixed woodland of Milton Park Wood and follow the path through the wood, continuing along the right-hand fork on joining a broad track. After about 100 yards (91 m), turn right onto a clear path that heads uphill and continues by the right-hand edge of the wood, before heading downhill into the wood again to a track. Turn right and then almost immediately left to follow a tarmac track up to a road. Cross the road and continue into a

SCALE 1:27 778 or 2¼ INCHES to 1 MILE

small housing estate. After about 50 yards (46 m), take the first turning on the left (between bungalows), turn right for a few yards, and then turn left along an enclosed path between wire fences. Head downhill through woodland (there are steps in places), turning right at the bottom to join a road (**D**).

Follow the road through the planned estate village of Milton Abbas. Its predecessor lay nearer Milton Abbey, but when Joseph Damer, later the first Lord Milton, bought the estate in 1752 and planned to build a house next to the abbey, he decided to demolish the original village because it would spoil his view. By a series of unscrupulous actions, he forced out all the inhabitants and had the new village built on the present site between 1773 and 1780. Despite such dubious and regrettable origins, the result is both of great historic interest and undeniably picturesque: a long and gently curving street lined by wide grass verges and two rows of virtually identical thatched cottages, with a thatched pub and small church providing the two most vital village amenities.

At the end of the village, turn right at a junction signposted to Milton Abbey. In front of a brick-built thatched cottage, bear left (**E**) at a public footpath sign to 'Milton Abbey, Church Only' along a path that keeps by the right-hand side of Milton Abbas Lake. Ahead is an attractive view of the abbey tower framed by trees. Continue to the abbey itself, which stands in a lovely setting amidst glorious landscaped parkland and surrounded by wooded hills. Joseph Damer demolished the monastic buildings to make way for his house, and the surviving church has an unusual uncompleted appearance. This is because after the Norman church was destroyed by fire in the early fourteenth century, a nave was never built for its successor; thus it comprises just the fourteenth-century choir, plus tower and transepts. Damer's great house next to it is now a public school.

Turn right onto a path by the south side of the abbey that winds along to a tarmac drive, and turn left to follow the drive through a car park to a road. Turn left (signposted to Hilton) and to the left is a magnificent view of the house and abbey across the school playing-fields. The road heads uphill to the edge of woodland where, at a bridleway sign, you turn right along a track (**F**). Pass beside a wooden barrier and continue along an uphill path through Thomas's Hill and Horse Park Plantations, more delightful woodland. After a while the path levels off and eventually curves left, heading uphill again to emerge from the wood and continue between bracken to a gate. Go through the gate to enter Green Hill Down Reserve, belonging to the Dorset Naturalists' Trust, and keep ahead across this lovely area of grassland, fringed by trees and with fine views to the right of wooded downland.

Continue along a tree-lined track, go through a metal gate, and keep along the left-hand edge of sloping meadows, by a hedge and wire fence on the left, passing through several more metal gates. An enclosed track between fences leads past Bulbarrow Farm, before you finally walk along a tarmac track by the left-hand edge of Delcombe Wood, the last of the many fine wooded areas encountered on this walk, to reach a road (**G**). Turn right, still keeping by the edge of Delcombe Wood, to return to the car park and viewpoint at the top of Bulbarrow Hill. □

24 Cranborne and the Allen valley

Start:	Cranborne
Distance:	9 miles (14.5 km)
Approximate time:	4½ hours
Parking:	Cranborne
Refreshments:	Pubs at Cranborne
Ordnance Survey maps:	Landranger 184 (Salisbury & The Plain) and 195 (Bournemouth & Purbeck), Pathfinder 1282, SU 01/11 (Fordingbridge)

General description *Most of the wild forest may have disappeared under the plough, but Cranborne Chase, a region of rolling chalk uplands interspersed with detached woodlands extending over much of north-east Dorset and adjoining areas of*

Wiltshire and Hampshire, still retains an aura of remoteness and loneliness. It is fine walking country, and this walk takes you through a typical chase landscape of sweeping views, wide open spaces and far horizons. Although a lengthy walk, the paths are good, the route is easy to follow and the gradients are gentle.

The former royal forest of Cranborne became a chase in the early seventeenth century, when James I bestowed it upon Robert Cecil, Earl of Salisbury. In the eighteenth and early nineteenth centuries it became a refuge for poachers and smugglers and was notorious for violence and lawlessness. In the heart of the chase is the small and peaceful village of Cranborne, once the chase's administrative centre and a place of considerable importance. Two buildings testify to its former greatness. One is the impressive church, sole survivor of a large priory, noted for its Norman south doorway, thirteenth-century nave and rare fourteenth-century wall-paintings. The other is Cranborne

Manor, one of the earliest domestic buildings in the country. Originally built as a hunting lodge by King John in the early thirteenth century, it was enlarged and modernised in the seventeenth century by Robert Cecil. The house is not open to the public, but its fine gardens sometimes are.

Start in The Square and turn along Crane Street (signposted Damerham). After a few yards, turn left and take the first turning on the right (Penny's Lane) at a public footpath sign to Jordan Hill. Walk along the right-hand edge of a playing-field, continue along a hedge-lined track and, after about 200 yards (183 m), turn left at a yellow waymark. Keep along the left-hand edge of a field, by a hedge on the left. From this path there are grand views over sweeping country dotted with belts of woodland.

On reaching a lane, turn right for a few yards and then turn left over a stile beside a metal gate (**A**) to follow a track into Burwood. After a few yards the main track bears right, but you keep ahead along a clear, grassy track that continues through this

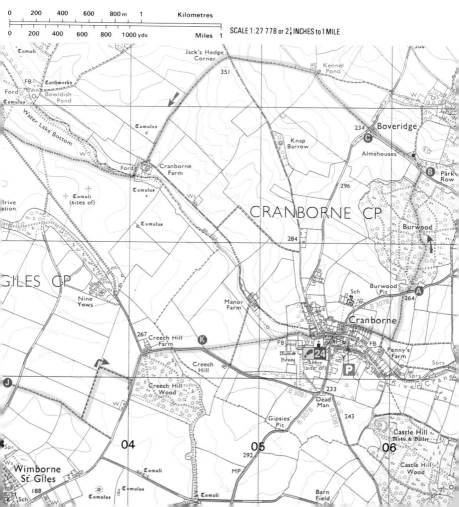

SCALE 1:27 778 or 2¼ INCHES to 1 MILE

An inviting path leads across fields to Cranborne Manor and church

lovely mixed woodland, a remnant of the extensive woods that once clothed Cranborne Chase, climbing a stile onto a lane (**B**). Turn left, follow the lane to a T-junction (**C**), and continue straight ahead along a track signposted to West Blagdon. On meeting another track in front of a barn, bear left along it and, at a fork a short distance ahead, take the left-hand track. At a crossroads of tracks, climb a stile and keep ahead gently downhill, passing through several metal gates, to Cranborne Farm.·

At the farm buildings turn right, go through a metal gate, turn left along a track, and climb a stile beside a metal gate. Bear left and then right to ford the little River Crane, and turn right through a blue-waymarked gate. Continue along a track that at first keeps parallel to the river but later bears gradually left away from it. Go through a metal gate and keep ahead towards the woodland on the horizon.

Go through a gate onto a road (**D**) and turn right along it for nearly ½ mile (0.75 km). (Take care: the traffic is fast and there are no verges.) At the end of a wooded lay-by on the left, turn sharp left (**E**) along a track through the trees, pass beside a waymarked barrier and continue along a very pleasant track, eventually heading downhill to a lane. Turn right into the hamlet of Monkton Up Wimborne, and opposite a post-box turn left along a hedge-lined track (**F**). The track at first heads steadily uphill before levelling off. About 100 yards (91 m) after passing a track on the right, turn left along a broad, stony track (**G**). Follow it downhill, passing a farm,

and continue along a tarmac track to a lane. Keep ahead along the lane and take the first turning on the left to continue along a narrower lane (**H**).

Cross a bridge over the River Allen and to the right is a fine view of the Georgian church of Wimborne St Giles. Head gently uphill for nearly ½ mile (0.75 km) and, where a track crosses the lane, turn right (**J**) along the track, between a hedge on the right and a wire fence on the left. Turn left at a yellow waymark, and look out for where another yellow waymark directs you to the right along a wide, grassy track between fields to a road. Just before reaching the road turn left and keep along the right-hand edge of a field, by a hedge bordering the road on the right. Turn right over a stile onto the road and continue along the lane ahead, signposted to Cranborne.

After ¼ mile (0.5 km), where the lane bends slightly to the right, climb a stile (**K**) at a footpath sign, and take the path straight ahead across a field. From here is a particularly striking view of Cranborne Manor and church appearing amongst the trees ahead. Climb a stile, cross a track, climb another stile, and continue across the next field, over another stile and along the right-hand edge of a meadow. Turn left over a concrete footbridge, then turn right and keep to the left of the hedge and fence bordering Cranborne Manor; at one point there is a fine view of the house. Climb two stiles in quick succession and continue along a tarmac drive into Cranborne, turning right back to The Square. ☐

25 The heart of 'Hardy Country'

Refer to map overleaf.

Start:	Higher Bockhampton: Thorncombe Wood and Black Heath car park, ½ mile (0.75 km) south of the A35 between Dorchester and Puddletown
Distance:	9 miles (14.5 km)
Approximate time:	4½ hours
Parking:	Thorncombe Wood and Black Heath car park
Refreshments:	None
Ordnance Survey maps:	Landranger 194 (Dorchester & Weymouth) and Pathfinder 1318, SY 69/79 (Dorchester (North) & Tolpuddle)

General description *Almost any walk in Dorset can claim to be in 'Hardy Country' as the entire county is associated with the writer. However, this walk is genuinely in the heart of 'Hardy Country' as it starts near the cottage in which Thomas Hardy was born and passes the churchyard in which his heart is buried. The route also includes attractive stretches of woodland, a fine ridge-top walk with extensive views, and a delightful stroll by the water-meadows of the River Frome, thus encompassing many of the features of the rich and varied landscape of his native county that Hardy so loved and which inspired so many of his works.*

From the car park take the path signposted 'Hardy's Cottage via Woodland Path' that heads immediately into woodland, winding uphill through the trees. At a signpost for Hardy's Cottage, turn left, and the path soon bends to the right and continues to the cottage itself. It was in this simple thatched cottage, built by his great-grandfather in 1800, that Thomas Hardy was born in 1840. It was also here that he wrote two of his best-known novels: *Under the Greenwood Tree* and *Far from the Madding Crowd*. Nowadays it is in the care of the National Trust.

At the cottage turn right (**A**), pass beside a wooden barrier by a blue waymark, and take the track that continues through the mixed woodland of Puddletown Forest. Keep ahead, following blue waymarks all the while, crossing two tracks and, after the second one, heading gently downhill. Continue through Tolpuddle Hollow to pass beside a barrier onto a lane and, just before reaching the lane, turn left (**B**) along an uphill wooded track lined by fine old beeches. Eventually, you emerge from the forest to reach the A35.

Carefully cross this busy road and go through a metal gate opposite, at a bridleway sign. Continue along an uphill, tree-lined, enclosed track. This is a very pleasant part of the walk, as the track climbs between more fine beeches and then gently descends to a T-junction of tracks, by a blue-waymarked post (**C**). Here turn left along a gently undulating hedge-lined track, the Ridge Way, and follow it for the next 1¾ miles (3 km), keeping more or less in a straight line. All the way there are fine views both sides over gently rolling country; later, to the left, Puddletown Forest and Dorchester can be seen, and the finest views of all come

The River Frome flows lazily between meadows near Lower Bockhampton in the heart of 'Hardy Country'

towards the end when the track climbs onto Waterston Ridge.

On reaching a road turn left (**D**) for a few yards and, opposite a bridleway sign to Charminster, turn left through a metal gate and head downhill across grass to join a wire fence. At this point the official right of way crosses the fence and continues across a field, but this is virtually impossible to follow because of the absence of a stile and obstruction by crops. Therefore it is easier to keep by the fence, following it around a right-hand bend and along to a pair of metal gates. Turn right through the first of these and walk along the left-hand edge of a field, by a metal fence on the left, keeping along the edge of several fields and passing through three metal gates, the last one to the left of a barn.

Now continue along a track lined by fences, go through another metal gate, and keep ahead along a concrete drive between farm buildings. Passing to the left of Kingston House, walk along a tarmac drive to the A35 (**E**).

Cross the road once more and go through a metal gate opposite. Turn right, in the direction of a bridleway sign, along the right-

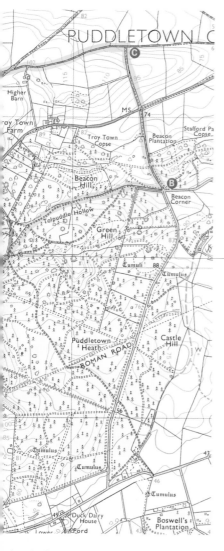

hand edge of the field, by a hedge and wire fence on the right. Ahead is a view of the façade of a large white house, Kingston Maurward, now the Dorset College of Agriculture and Horticulture. Go through a metal gate, follow a track across a field to a lane (**F**) and turn right along it for ½ mile (0.75 km).

At a signpost to 'Stinsford Church and Stinsford School', turn left (**G**) along a narrow lane and follow it into the village. The lane passes to the left of the secluded churchyard, although its tranquillity is now somewhat shattered by the noise of traffic from the A35, in which Hardy's heart is buried, as are both his wives, several members of his family, and the poet Cecil Day Lewis. Hardy's ashes were buried at Poets' Corner in Westminster Abbey. Stinsford church is a lovely, simple little building, dating mainly from the thirteenth century.

Continue along a tarmac track, which later becomes a narrow tree-lined path, and at a T-junction turn left (**H**) to walk along another delightful tree-lined path that forms a causeway raised above the meadows bordering the River Frome, with streams on both sides. Cross one of the branches of the river and keep alongside it to a lane and bridge.

Turn left to cross the bridge into the hamlet of Lower Bockhampton, where Hardy briefly attended school, and take the first turning on the right (**J**). Pass between farm buildings and, where the track bends to the right, go through the yellow-waymarked gate in front. Keep ahead across a field (there is no visible path) and to the right is a lovely view of the placid Frome, winding lazily between meadows that can have changed little over the centuries. Climb a stile on the far side of the field, just to the left of woodland, and continue along the right-hand edge of the next field, by trees on the right, later bearing left away from the field-edge towards a house. Keeping to the left of the house, go through a metal gate and turn left along a track. Cross a lane and keep ahead towards the dark woodlands of Puddletown Forest, passing to the right of a farm. Continue through several gates before entering the woodlands.

At a crossroads of paths and tracks, turn left (**K**) off the main track to follow a path along the left-hand edge of Black Heath which, together with neighbouring Thorncombe Wood, is a Dorset County Council wildlife sanctuary adjoining the Forestry Commission's Puddletown Forest. Now comes a lovely finale to the walk: at first along the edge of the forest with fine, open views to the left across fields, and later through the attractive and peaceful Thorncombe Wood. At a fork bear right along a path that heads downhill into woodland, and at the bottom turn left to join a track. The track bears right to pass through a small picnic area and continues to the car park and starting point. □

26 Beaminster, Netherbury and Lewesdon Hill

Start:	Beaminster
Distance:	8 miles (12.75 km)
Approximate time:	4 hours
Parking:	Beaminster
Refreshments:	Pubs and cafés at Beaminster, pub at Stoke Abbott
Ordnance Survey maps:	Landranger 193 (Taunton & Lyme Regis), Pathfinders 1298, ST 40/50 (Crewkerne & Beaminster) and 1317, SY 49/59 (Bridport)

General description *The route takes you through the hilly country of west Dorset that lies to the south and west of Beaminster. There is plenty of uphill work, but the climbs are steady rather than steep or strenuous. The paths are generally good, but between Netherbury and Stoke Abbott there are some places where the route is not clearly defined and there is one particularly overgrown ½-mile (0.75 km) stretch. Adequate footwear and a careful scrutiny of the route directions will overcome these minor difficulties and enable you to enjoy a walk of tremendous variety and outstanding scenery.*

The pleasant old town of Beaminster is dominated by its imposing fifteenth-century church. Start in the square by the market cross and walk down Church Street. Turn left along St Mary Well Street which, after the last of the houses, becomes a rough track. Where the track turns left, keep ahead along a grassy path that heads gently uphill, by woodland on the left. Go through a gate, follow the direction of a bridleway sign straight across a field and, at the far end, keep ahead by a hedge on the right.

Climb a stile and immediately the paths fork (**A**): the main route continues ahead, but a brief detour along the left-hand track, heading downhill and crossing a footbridge over the River Brit, allows you to visit Parnham House, built in the sixteenth century but extensively remodelled in the eighteenth and early nineteenth centuries.

Return to the main route and turn sharp left at the path junction (keep ahead if omitting the detour) and walk along the right-hand edge of woodland, later joining a track. Look out for and turn right over a waymarked stile beside a gate, immediately turn left, climb another stile, and continue along a hedge-lined track. After a few yards the track bears right, but you keep ahead along a path to climb a stile and continue along the left-hand edge of a field, by trees on the left. Go through a gate to enter woodland, and on emerging from the wood continue along a hedge-lined path to the left of Netherbury church, curving right to reach a lane (**B**).

Turn right along the lane, passing in front of the fourteenth-century church. Follow the lane around a left-hand bend, bear right to go through a waymarked metal gate, and continue along the left-hand edge of a field, passing to the right of a house, to a stile. From now on there are grand views of the arc of hills that are either climbed or passed by on the later stages of the walk: Lewesdon Hill in front, and to the right Waddon Hill, with Gerrard's Hill further right still.

Climb the stile, keep ahead for a few yards, and turn right to go through a gate. Continue along a path, between a fence bordering stables and a riding school to the left and a hedge on the right, to another gate. Go through that, turn right to climb the stile ahead, and walk steeply downhill along a fence-lined path. At the bottom comes the first difficulty. Continue through an area of trees and scrub (the path may be boggy and slightly overgrown), cross over two narrow

brooks, and continue to a stile on the edge of the trees. There are several overgrown paths in this area of scrub and trees, which can be slightly confusing; it is most important that you leave the trees via a stile and not by a gate.

Climb the stile, head uphill across the sloping meadow in front, keeping by a wire fence on the right and making for a metal gate. Go through to reach the second and last difficult part. For the next ½ mile (0.75 km) you walk along a very overgrown, hedge-lined track, heading gently uphill. It is a bit of a battle, but persevere and the rest of the route presents no difficulties at all. You have to be careful where you leave this track; just before it curves to the left, turn right off it. The path is difficult to spot because it is almost hidden by scrub, but an additional landmark is an area of trees to the right. After a few yards, this narrow and overgrown path leads to a metal gate; go through this and bear left downhill across a field, keeping roughly parallel to the field edge on the left.

Cross a brook at the bottom, climb a waymarked stile in front, and head uphill across rough pasture, keeping in the same direction, to enter Stoke Abbott churchyard. Turn right through a metal gate to leave the churchyard, and take a path that bears left and continues to a lane in the centre of Stoke Abbott (**C**), another sleepy and largely unchanged village of stone and thatched cottages.

The pub is to the right; to continue the walk, turn left and, at the end of the village, the lane bends to the right. Continue along it for 1 mile (1.5 km) between high embankments on both sides, following the lane around two sharp left-hand bends and one sharp right-hand bend (the latter by a farm), to reach a crossroads (**D**). Turn right and, just before the road curves to the right, turn left along a concrete track, signposted Lower Brimley Coombe Farm, heading uphill towards some of the stately beeches that clothe the slopes of Lewesdon Hill.

Where the drive broadens out, turn right through a metal gate along a path that heads uphill, soon bearing left and continuing upwards along the right-hand edge of woodland, by a hedge-bank crowned by a line of grand old beeches on the right. Now comes a section through beautiful woodland of widely spaced oaks and beeches, with magnificent views through gaps in the trees on the right. Continue past a National Trust sign for Lewesdon Hill, now climbing more steeply to reach the flat, tree-clad summit, the site of an Iron Age hill-fort, from which there are more superb panoramic views.

Ahead are two grassy paths; take the right-hand one, which soon starts to head downhill to reach a junction of tracks and paths by another National Trust sign. Here turn right onto a track that keeps along the edge of woodland, later continuing as a sunken track between hedge-banks (muddy in places),

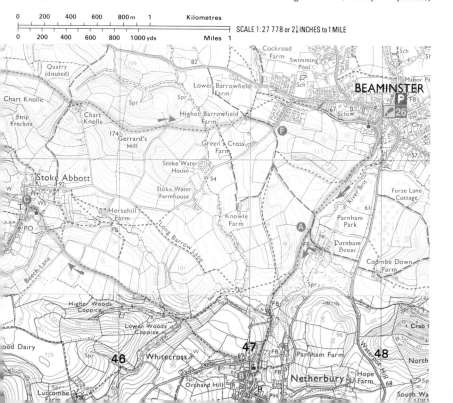

SCALE 1:27 778 or 2¼ INCHES to 1 MILE

heading downhill and finally curving left to a road (**E**).

Cross the road and go through a metal gate at a public footpath sign to Beaminster. This brings you into a farmyard. Walk between farm buildings to two metal gates ahead. Go through the right-hand one (yellow waymark) and initially keep along the left-hand edge of a field, by a wire fence on the left, later following the track as it curves right up to another pair of metal gates. Again go through the right-hand one and continue along the left-hand edge of a field, by a wire fence on the left, below the ridge of Waddon Hill on the right, which is crowned by a small Roman fort. Go through a metal gate, keep along the left-hand edge of the next field, go through another metal gate, and continue along a pleasant green track just above a hedge on the left.

Descend slightly to pass through a hedge gap and continue, now by a hedge on the right, along a flat, broad, grassy ledge. Go through a metal gate in front of a house, bear left and then right to pass to the left of the house, turn right through a metal gate where the wall on the right ends, and turn half-left to head uphill across rough grass to another metal gate. Go through and continue by a hedge on the left, climbing steadily towards the summit of Gerrard's Hill. You will pass through a metal gate to keep ahead to the tree-clad summit. From here the all-round view is magnificent: an extensive panorama over downs, hills and woods.

Passing to the left of the triangulation pillar, continue ahead for about 100 yards (91 m) and then veer slightly left to head downhill along a ridge, joining and keeping by a wire fence on the left, to a stile. Climb this, cross a track, go through the metal gate opposite, and follow the direction of a waymark straight ahead steeply downhill across a field, making for a footbridge at the bottom. Cross this, head across the field in front to pass through a hedge gap, and continue uphill across the next field to a stile. Climb the stile and head across the next field towards a farmhouse, bearing slightly left to climb yet another stile.

Now keep ahead to go through a metal gate to the left of the farmhouse and continue along the track in front to a lane (**F**). Turn left down the lane into Beaminster, passing modern housing on the edge of the town, and just before reaching the main road, turn right through a kissing-gate to follow a pleasant green path across a meadow, with the tower of the church directly ahead. At the end of the meadow, climb a stile and continue along a hedge-lined track. Later this becomes a lane which passes to the left of the church. Bear left to return to the square in the town centre. □

27 Kimmeridge Bay and Swyre Head

Start:	Kimmeridge
Distance:	8½ miles (13.5 km)
Approximate time:	5 hours
Parking:	Kimmeridge – car park just to north-east above village
Refreshments:	Café at Kimmeridge, pub at Kingston
Ordnance Survey maps:	Landranger 195 (Bournemouth & Purbeck) and Outdoor Leisure 15 (Purbeck)

General description *After an initial short walk across fields from Kimmeridge to reach the sea, the route continues for 3 miles (4.75 km) along a particularly attractive stretch of coast, before turning inland to*

SCALE 1:27 778 or 2¼ INCHES to 1 MILE

Kingston. Then comes a gradual climb to the superb viewpoint at Swyre Head and finally an exhilarating walk along a downland ridge. Magnificent views along the whole length of the Purbeck coastline, from the Isle of Portland in the west to Poole Harbour in the east, plus equally grand views inland looking across to the Purbeck ridge, make this an outstanding walk, with only one fairly steep climb.

A grassy path descends into Kimmeridge

From the car park above Kimmeridge, turn right along the lane to a junction a few yards ahead and turn left over a stile at a public footpath sign to Kimmeridge. A pleasant, grassy path heads downhill into the village, with fine views of the coast ahead. Go through a metal kissing-gate into the churchyard and walk through it, passing to the left of the small, plain Victorian church. Go through another metal kissing-gate and continue along the lane, lined with thatched stone cottages, through the village.

Look out for a stile on the right, where a notice says 'Footpath to the Sea' (**A**), climb it and walk along the right-hand edge of a field, by a wire fence on the right. Cross a footbridge and turn left to keep along the left-hand edge of a field, by a hedge on the left, continuing along the meandering left-hand edge of a number of fields and climbing several stiles to emerge eventually onto a lane (**B**). Turn left at a footpath sign to 'Beach and Coast Path', and shortly turn right across a car park to the low cliffs above Kimmeridge

Bay, before turning left to join the coast path. Follow the curve of the bay to a rough tarmac track, turn right along it and, at a 'Coast Path' sign, turn left up a flight of steps to ascend Hen Cliff.

At the top you pass the prominent landmark of Clavell's Tower, erected in the early nineteenth century and now a ruin. Keep along the top of the cliffs for the next 3 miles (4.75 km), a particularly attractive stretch of coast with spectacular views towards St Aldhelm's Head and passing the Kimmeridge Ledges at the base of the shale cliffs. Although undulating, this is a fairly easy section of the coast path, the most strenuous part being the steep ascent of Houns-tout Cliff after descending into Egmont Bight, where a waterfall drops into the sea. At the top of Houns-tout Cliff, a

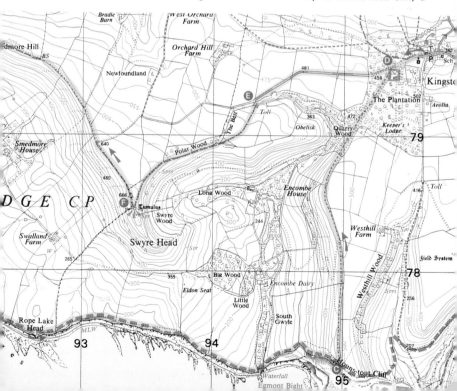

strategically placed stone seat allows you to enjoy extensive views along the whole of the Purbeck coast in both directions: from the Isle of Portland in the west to Poole Harbour and the coast of Hampshire in the east.

By the stone seat and a footpath marker-stone to Kingston a few yards ahead, turn left (**C**), climb a stile, and walk along a very pleasant, broad, grassy ledge, keeping parallel to a wall on the right and climbing several stiles. To the left are views over Encombe valley and later on Encombe House can be seen. Continue along a tree-lined track, by the right-hand edge of Quarry Wood, and on through the Plantation; keeping along the main track and following signs to Kingston all the while, to emerge onto a lane (**D**). Turn sharp left along the lane if continuing on the main route, but turn right for a brief detour into the village of Kingston, which boasts two nineteenth-century churches as well as stone cottages and a pub. The original medieval church, now redundant, was rebuilt in the 1830s, but in the 1870s a new, large, ornate church, almost cathedral-like, was provided for the village by the 3rd Earl of Eldon of nearby Encombe House. It was designed by George Edmund Street, one of the foremost Victorian architects.

Retrace your steps to rejoin the main route and continue along the lane for ¾ mile (1.25 km). At first the lane runs through woodland, but it soon emerges into open country with extensive views. The views to the right are particularly impressive, looking across to the Purbeck ridge and Corfe Castle.

On reaching a small car park on the left, turn left (**E**) between stone gateposts and bear right to go through a blue-waymarked gate. Walk along a track across open grassland, pass through a gate, and the track continues along the left-hand edge of Polar Wood, heading steadily uphill and curving left to reach Swyre Head (**F**). Even by the standards of this walk, the all-round views from the tumulus are outstanding: the whole length of the Purbeck coast and inland over the Purbeck ridge to the forests and heathlands around Poole Harbour.

At Swyre Head turn right (footpath marker-stone to Smedmore Hill and Kimmeridge), walk past a triangulation pillar, and go through the gate beyond. Now continue along a splendid high-level track over Smedmore Hill, keeping by a wall on the left all the while. The route passes through several metal gates and all the way there are more outstanding views both over the coast and inland, a superb finale. The track finally descends to a lane, where you turn left to a junction, turning left again to the car park a few yards ahead. □

74

28 The Hardy Monument and Maiden Castle

Start:	Hardy Monument – ¾ mile (1.25 km) east of the road between Portesham and the A35
Distance:	9 ½ miles (15.25 km). Shorter version 8 ½ miles (13.5 km)
Approximate time:	5 hours (4 hours for shorter version)
Parking:	Hardy Monument
Refreshments:	Pub at Martinstown
Ordnance Survey maps:	Landranger 194 (Dorchester & Weymouth) and Pathfinder 1332, SY 68/78 (Weymouth (North) & Dorchester (South))

General description *The starting point by the Hardy Monument, a commanding viewpoint high up on the wind-swept downs, sets the tone for this splendid walk, mostly along broad, downland ridges and through dry, valley bottoms, across an open and largely deserted countryside studded with reminders of prehistoric man. At the halfway point, you pass one of the most extensive, impressive and best-preserved Iron Age forts in the country, well worth a thorough exploration. Although a lengthy walk with plenty of ups and downs, the terrain is neither difficult nor strenuous, and all the ascents and descents are gradual. The shorter version of the walk gives you the option of returning to the start from point G.*

Refer to map overleaf.

In a county where it is impossible to escape from Hardy's pervading presence, it comes as a surprise to find that the Hardy Monument, erected on the summit of Black Down in 1844, has nothing to do with Thomas Hardy the writer but commemorates Admiral Sir Thomas Hardy, Nelson's right-hand man at the Battle of Trafalgar, who was born nearby.

Start at the monument with your back to the sea and take the narrow path ahead down to the road. Cross over and continue along the path opposite which bears right and heads downhill, between bracken and heather, bearing right again to rejoin the road. Turn left downhill and, at a signpost to Osmington Mills and Corton Hill, turn right (**A**) along a broad track, following it for nearly 1 mile (1.5 km) along a ridge, from which there are wide and spectacular views across the downs and to the sea. Just after going through the second of two metal gates, bear left at a junction of tracks, signposted to Martinstown (**B**).

Follow a track across the open downland, joining and keeping by a wire fence on the right. Go through a metal gate and around a right-hand bend, then curve slightly left and pass between tumuli to reach another metal gate at a footpath sign. Go through and turn left along a broad tarmac track, signposted to Martinstown, heading downhill. At the bottom of the hill, keep to the right of a house, bear right in front of a barn and shortly afterwards, at another footpath sign to Martinstown, turn right along a rough track. This track curves to the left, but you immediately leave it to go through a metal gate in front. Passing to the right of farm buildings, continue along an uphill grassy track and, where it levels off, keep alongside a wire fence on the right to a metal gate.

Go through the gate and continue straight ahead along a faint, grassy path, amidst a glorious rolling landscape, keeping just below the top of a bank and finally descending gently to go through a gate, by a footpath sign, onto a track. Cross the track and turn left across the grass, keeping parallel to the track and making for a fence corner. Here you pick up a discernible path and follow it, by a wire fence on the left, through Grove Hill Bottom to a gate. Go through, head uphill between newly planted conifers, go through another gate, and follow a path across a field, keeping parallel to a hedge on the right. At a footpath sign, go through a gate to join a tarmac track and follow it downhill into Martinstown, coming out into the village opposite the mainly fifteenth-century church (**C**).

Turn right along the road beside a stream and, at a blue-waymarked bridleway sign, turn left along an uphill tarmac track between houses. Turn right through a blue-way-marked metal gate, and walk along the right-hand edge of a field, by a wire fence bordering gardens. At the end of the field, go through a gate and continue along the edge of the next field, now by a line of fine old trees on the right, to pass through a metal gate onto a lane. Turn right to a junction, cross the road, and continue along the track opposite, heading gently uphill between a hedge on the left and a wire fence on the right, to a farm.

Pass between the farm buildings, go through a metal gate, turn right and then immediately turn left to pass in front of the house. Keep ahead between more farm buildings, curving left around the end of them, turn right through another metal gate and, after passing in front of another house, continue along a broad, straight track. Ahead the houses of Dorchester can be seen, but to the right the view is dominated by the mighty ramparts of Maiden Castle. Go through a metal gate to a crossroads of tracks and turn right uphill (**D**). The track later turns left to a metal gate. Go through this and turn right, immediately passing through another gate and continuing along a straight uphill track, bordered by gorse bushes on the right and running below the earthworks of the fort on the left.

A gate on the left admits you to Maiden Castle, one of the greatest prehistoric forts in Europe, enclosing an area of around 47 acres and with massive triple ramparts over 60 ft

The extensive and impressive earthworks of Maiden Castle are easily accessible

(18 m) high. It was the headquarters of the Durotriges tribe and at its peak housed between four and five thousand people. A bloody battle was fought here in AD 69 between the Durotriges and the Roman invaders and after the victory of the Romans, many of the defenders were slaughtered. After this the fort declined and was superseded by the new Roman town of Durnovaria (Dorchester). In the eastern part of the fort the Romans built a temple in the late fourth century, the foundations of which can still be seen.

The track soon heads downhill, continuing through a metal gate to run straight ahead towards the valley bottom. Go through a metal gate to join a lane and keep along it for ¼ mile (0.5 km) to a road.

Bear left along the road and shortly bear right (**E**), at a bridleway sign to Ridge Hill, along a tarmac drive, passing in front of a row of cottages. Continue between farm buildings to go through two waymarked metal gates in quick succession. The official right of way continues through a third gate but walkers will find it easier to turn right along an uphill track that later bends to the left and flattens out to reach a metal gate. Go through this and bear right to keep along the right-hand edge of a field, by a wire fence on the right, following the field edge round to the left for a few yards before turning right through a metal gate. Now turn half-left, head straight across the middle of a field (there is no visible path), passing to the left of a row of prominent tumuli, go through a metal gate in the far corner, and keep ahead to a junction of tracks.

Continue in the same direction across the field ahead (no path), heading uphill and making for a metal gate just to the right of two tumuli (**F**). Do not go through the gate, but turn right along the field edge, keeping by a wall on the left. There are grand sweeping views all round and the Hardy Monument can be seen on the hill directly ahead. Bear right to pass between two tumuli, then bear left to go through a metal gate and follow a track

along the edge of the next field, by a wall on the left, passing more tumuli. Go through a gate and continue along a grassy path, by a wire fence on the left, later joining and continuing along a stony track. Pass through the next metal gate (**G**).

For the shorter version of the walk keep along the clear track ahead to return to the start.

Turn left onto a narrow path, which squeezes between a wall on the left and gorse bushes on the right, to a stile and footpath sign to Corton Hill and Coryates. Climb the stile and head downhill along the right-hand edge of a field, by a wire fence and hedge on the right. At the bottom of the field turn right over a stile, immediately climb another, bear left across the corner of a field, and turn left along a downhill track.

About 100 yards (91 m) before reaching a road, turn right (**H**) along a track, by a wire fence and broken wall on the left. Soon you turn left through a metal gate and then turn right to continue, now with hedge and wall on the right. Go through a metal gate to continue through Hell Bottom, a totally unsuitable name for a delightful section of the walk on a pleasant, short-cropped, springy grass path, surrounded by superb downland scenery and with the Hardy Monument conspicuous on the skyline ahead most of the time. Keep in a straight line through a series of metal gates, climbing steadily in the later stages and continuing up to the brow of a hill, where you make for a gate to the right of a bank of gorse.

Go through onto a track and turn left to retrace your steps uphill to the Hardy Monument.   □

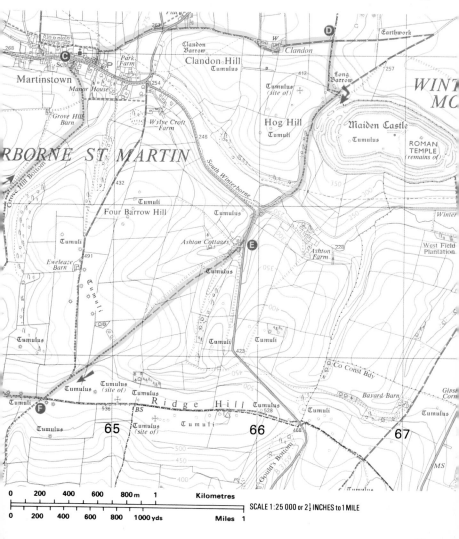

Useful organisations

The Countryside Commission
John Dower House, Crescent Place,
Cheltenham, Gloucestershire GL50 3RA.
Tel: 0242 21381

The National Trust
36 Queen Anne's Gate, London
SW1H 9AS. Tel: 071 222 9251
(Wessex Regional Office, Eastleigh
Court, Bishopstrow, Warminster,
Wiltshire BA12 9HW. Tel: 0985 847777)

West Country Tourist Board
37 Southernhay East, Exeter, Devon
EX1 1QS. Tel: 0392 76351

Southern Tourist Board
Town Hall Centre, Leigh Road,
Eastleigh, Hampshire, SO5 4DE.
Tel: 0703 221106

The Ramblers' Association
1/5 Wandsworth Road, London SW8 2LJ.
Tel: 071 582 6878

The Forestry Commission
Information Branch, 231 Corstorphine
Road, Edinburgh EH12 7AT.
Tel: 031 334 0303

The Youth Hostels Association
Trevelyan House, 8 St Stephen's Hill,
St Albans, Hertfordshire AL1 2DY.
Tel: 0727 55215

The Long Distance Walkers' Association
7 Ford Drive, Yarnfield, Stone,
Staffordshire ST15 0RP.
Tel: 0785 760684

The Council for the Protection of Rural
England, 25 Buckingham Palace Road,
London SW1W 0PP. Tel: 071 976 6433

Ordnance Survey
Romsey Road, Maybush, Southampton
SO9 4DH. Tel: 0703 792763/4 or 792792

Ordnance Survey maps of Dorset

Dorset is covered by Ordnance Survey
1:50 000 (1¼ inches to 1 mile) scale
Landranger map sheets 183, 184, 193, 194
and 195. These all-purpose maps are packed
with information to help you explore the area.
Viewpoints, picnic sites, places of interest,
caravan and camping sites are shown, as well
as public rights of way information such as
footpaths and bridleways.

To examine Dorset in more detail, and
especially if you are planning walks,
Ordnance Survey Pathfinder maps at
1:25 000 (2½ inches to 1 mile) scale are
ideal. Maps covering this area are:

1260 (ST 62/72)	1301 (SU 00/SZ 09)
1261 (ST 82/92)	1316 (SY 29/39)
1279 (ST 41/51)	1317 (SY 49/59)
1280 (ST 61/71)	1318 (SY 69/79)
1281 (ST 81/91)	1319 (SY 89/99)
1282 (SU 01/11)	1331 (SY 58)
1297 (ST 20/30)	1332 (SY 68/78)
1298 (ST 40/50)	1333 (SY 88/98)
1299 (ST 60/70)	1334 (SZ 08)
1300 (ST 80/90)	1343 (SY 67/77)

Outdoor Leisure maps 15 (Purbeck) and 22
(New Forest) cover parts of Dorset and are
also at 1:25 000 (2½ inches to 1 mile) scale.

To get to Dorset, use the Ordnance Survey
Routemaster maps number 8 (South West
England and South Wales) and number 9
(South East England) at 1:250 000 (1 inch to
4 miles) scale.

Ordnance Survey maps and guides are
available from most booksellers, stationers
and newsagents.

Index